PRACTICE

by

GARY LLAMA

OVOLR! / DEBACKLE
Richmond, Virginia
USA

Library of Congress Control Number: 2025951349

ISBN 979-8-9909185-9-7

OVOLR! / DEBACKLE
Richmond, Virginia USA

Practice?

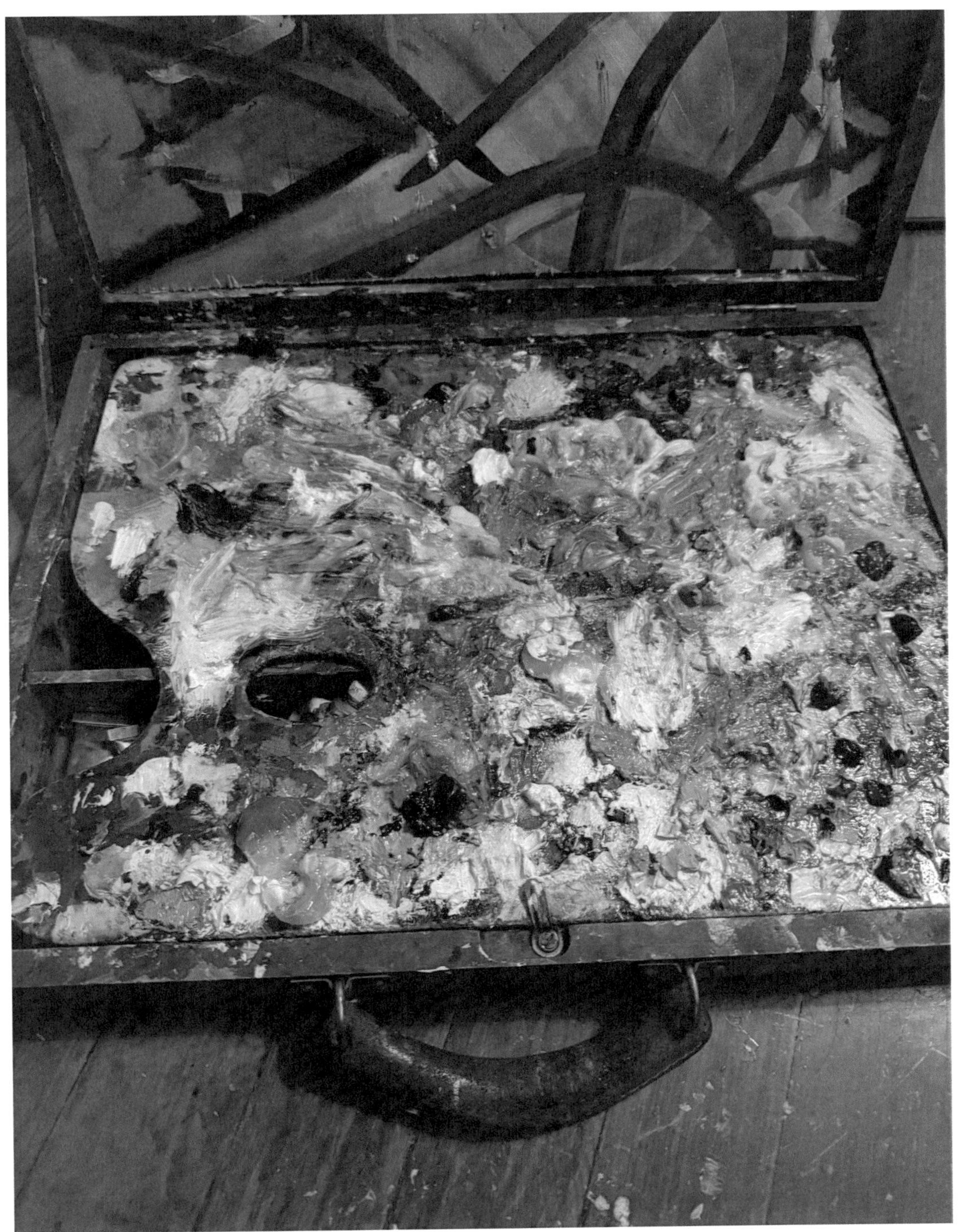

*The palette of my painting
box, passed down to me from
my Grandmother.*

As a person who creates things, a decision must be made at some point in that person's creative life: is the goal product, or process? And as an artist, my personal answer has shifted, from 'product', as a younger person, to 'process'.

The reasons for this shift, have as much to do with the work, as they do with my personal life and health. To live fully as an artist, making art itself, would seem to be a part of an artist's daily life, or at least close to it. However, for much of my life, art was something I did as relief, like a blow-off valve on a steam pipe, coming into play only at the last possible second.

There are reasons for this. Personally, as I grew and developed, and as my art grew and developed, art became more serious. These 'works' became 'work', and the act of painting, became methodical, and a motion of work itself.

But after some reflection about what I value in life, I realized that the idea of 'practice', was much closer to something I wanted as a part of my day. The idea of practice has less boundaries, less expectation, and accordingly,

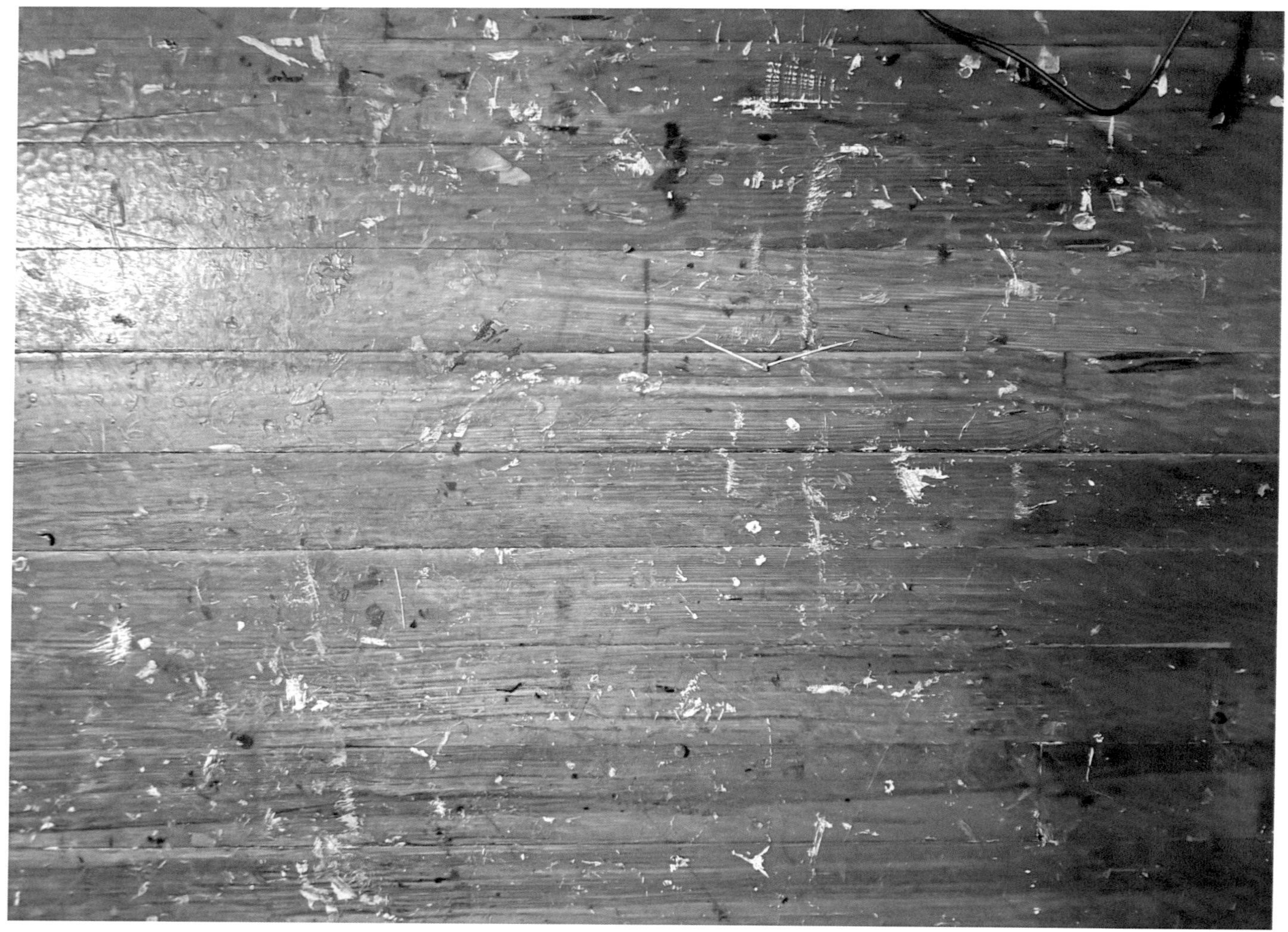

more room for experimentation.

And so as I began trying to paint multiple times per week, my art changed. And my life changed as well.

The place of painting became more casual as well, forgoing a studio, or even a formal spot, to me transforming my 'living room', into a multidisciplinary studio, for both my audio engineering and visual works.

And with these changes, both structurally in life, and in my mind and approach, I am producing much more work now., with much greater joy and ease.

While these paintings may not be the highest of my skill or time level I *could* achieve if I used someone else's methods, or model of living, they fit perfectly into my life. And each painting holds bits of my joys and fascinations,

as well as my idiosyncracies: each now fully being a product of my process, and a life I enjoy.

What follows in these pages, is a catalog of these paintings, spanning the past few years. Each made as a method of a mediation, of a practice now inherent in my daily life.

Gary Llama
12/22/2025

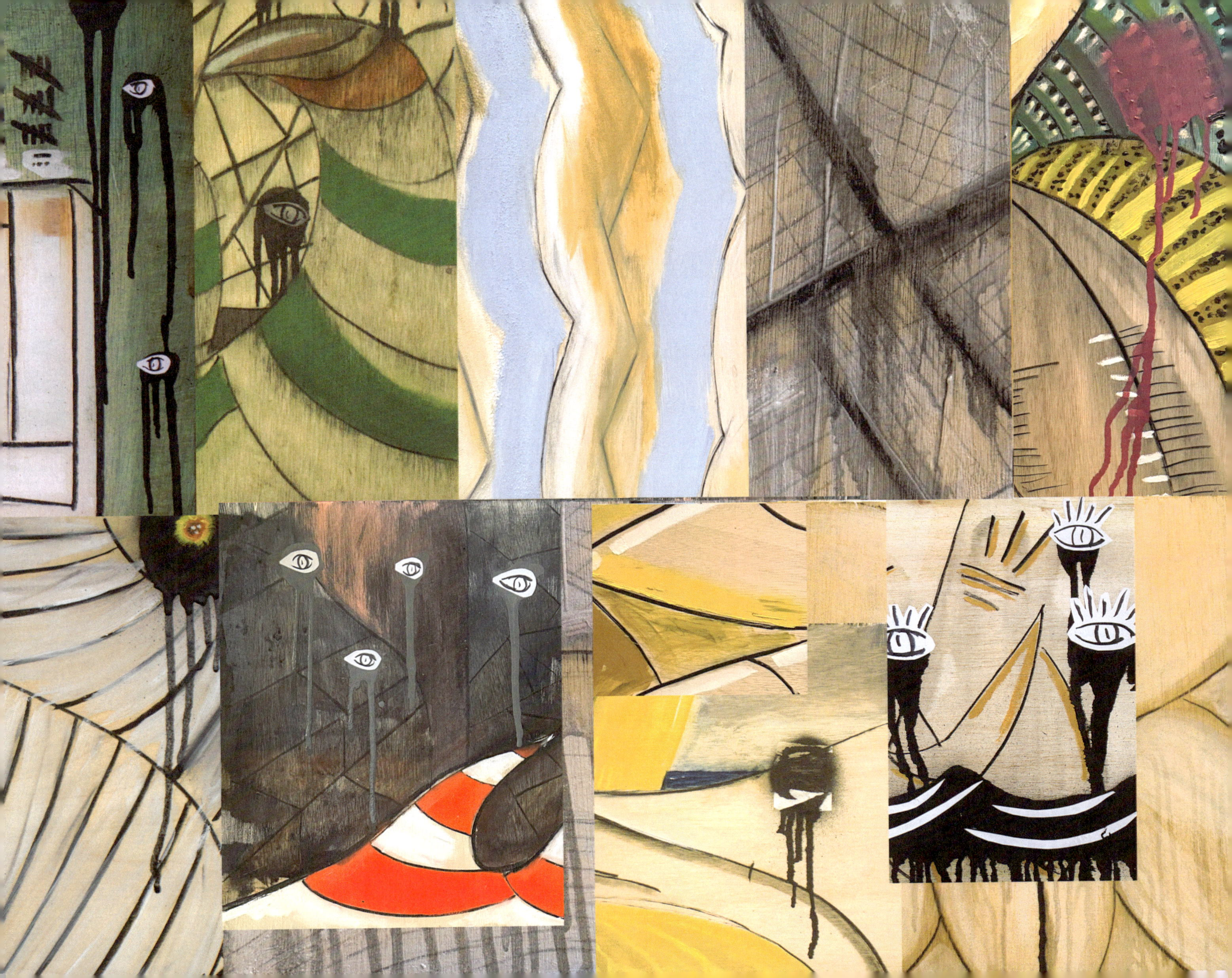

PRACTICE

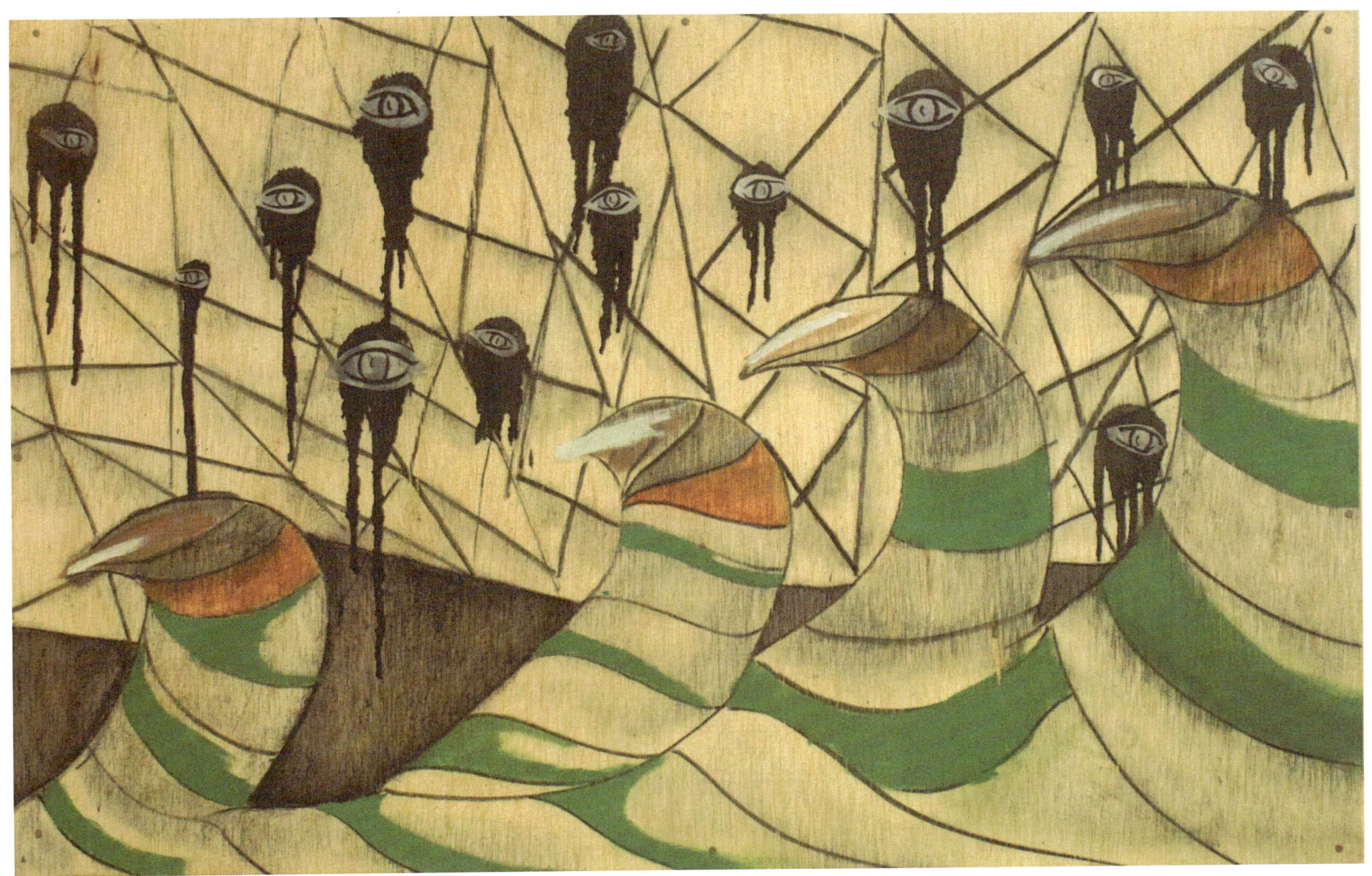

Wires

Oil, ink, paper, laquer, charcoal, on
wood panel
16"x24"
2023

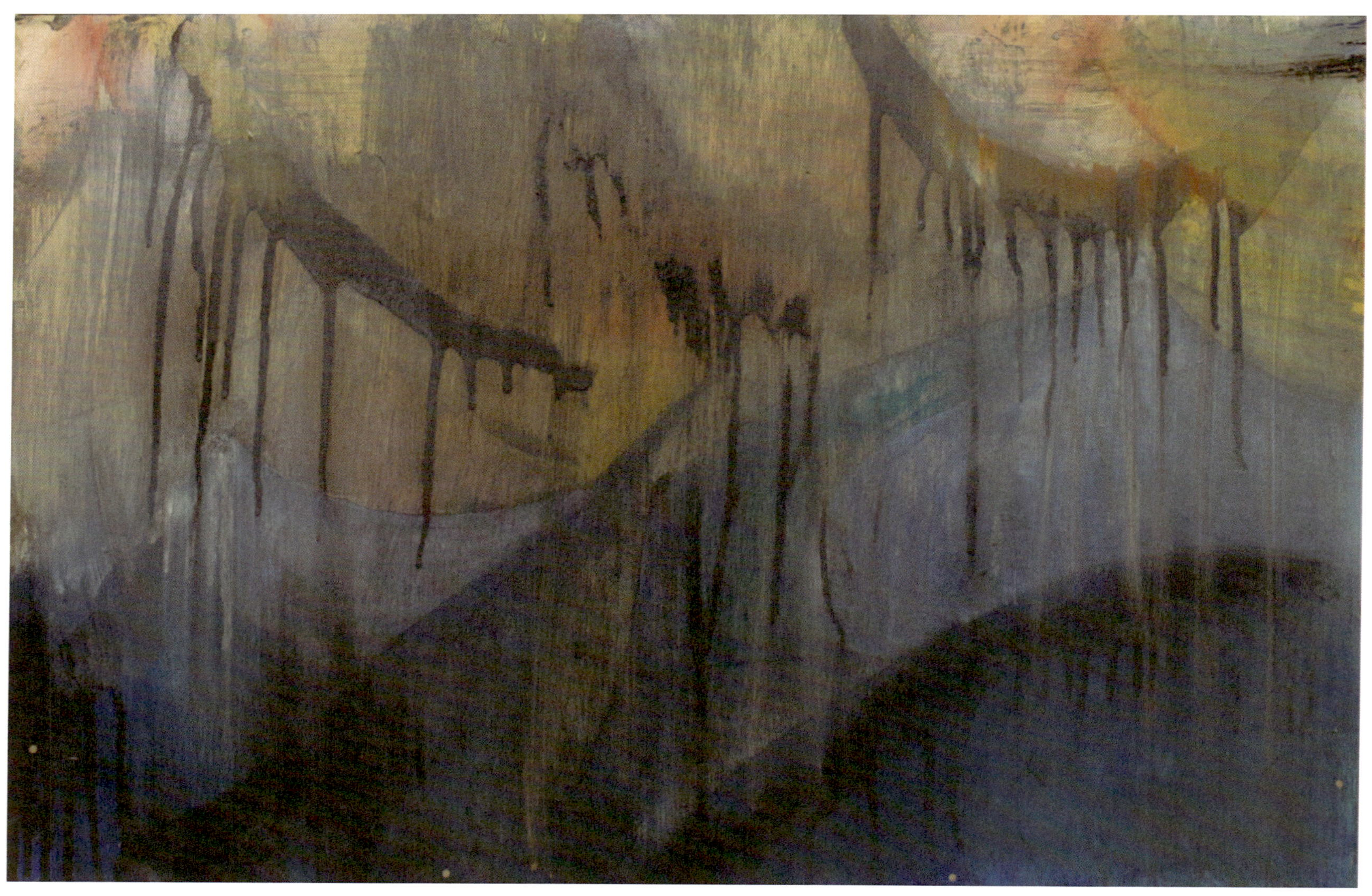

Sad Rock

Oil, Aerosol, graphite on wood panel
16"x24"
2023

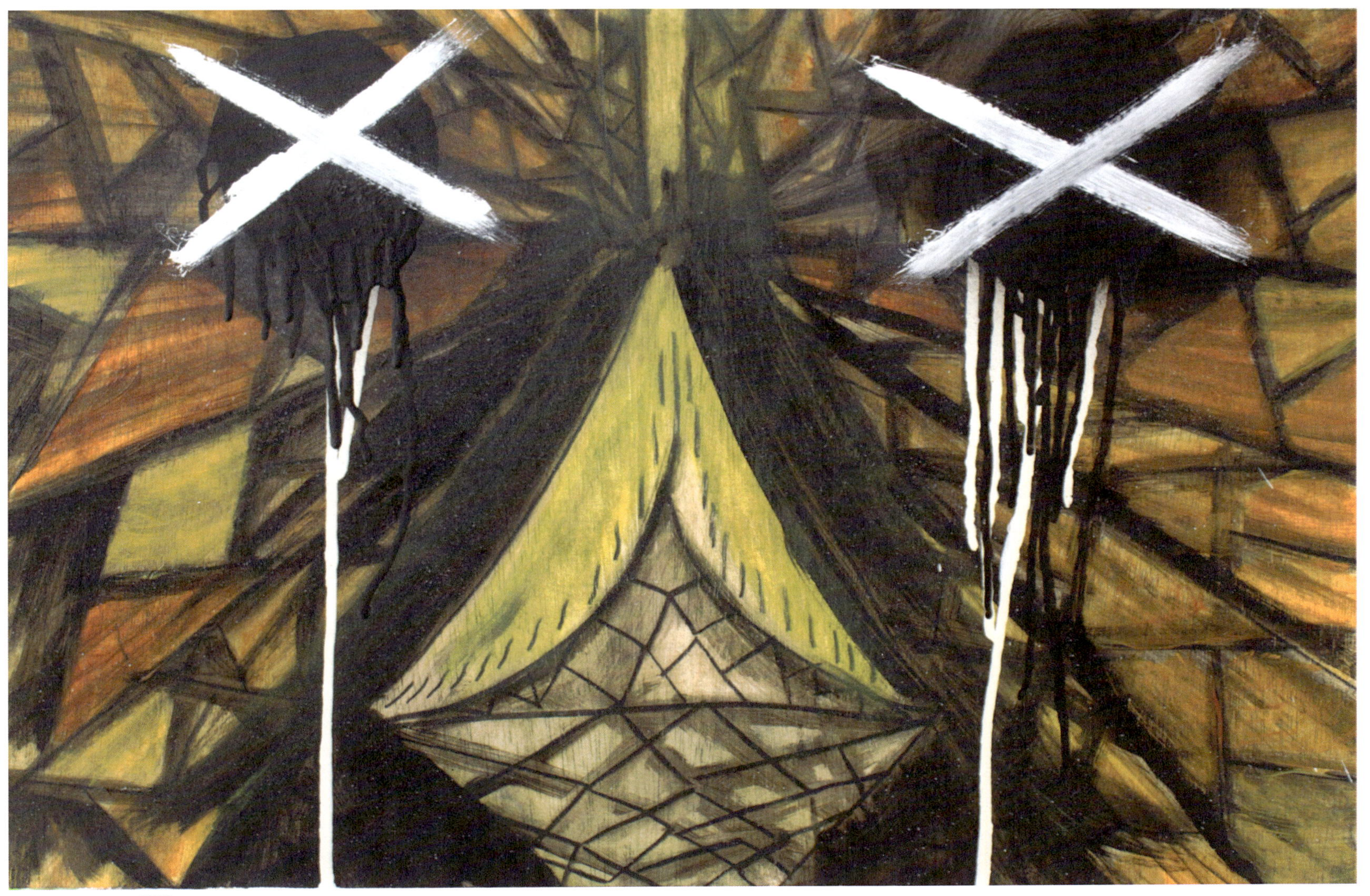

XXr

Oil, charcoal, aerosol, on wood
panel
16"x24"
2023

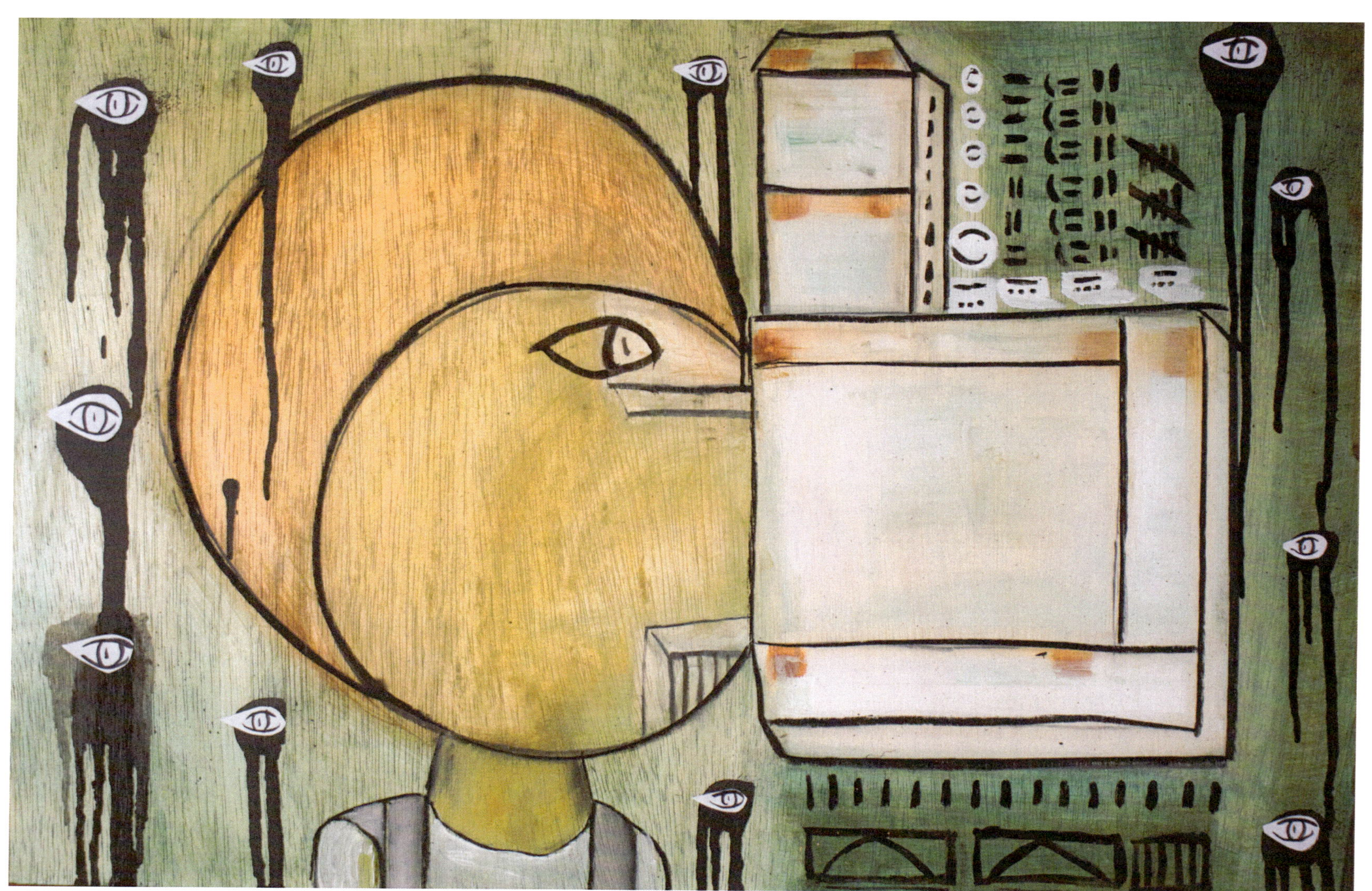

Multi-Ohm

Oil, aerosol, charcoal, on wood panel
16"x24"
2023

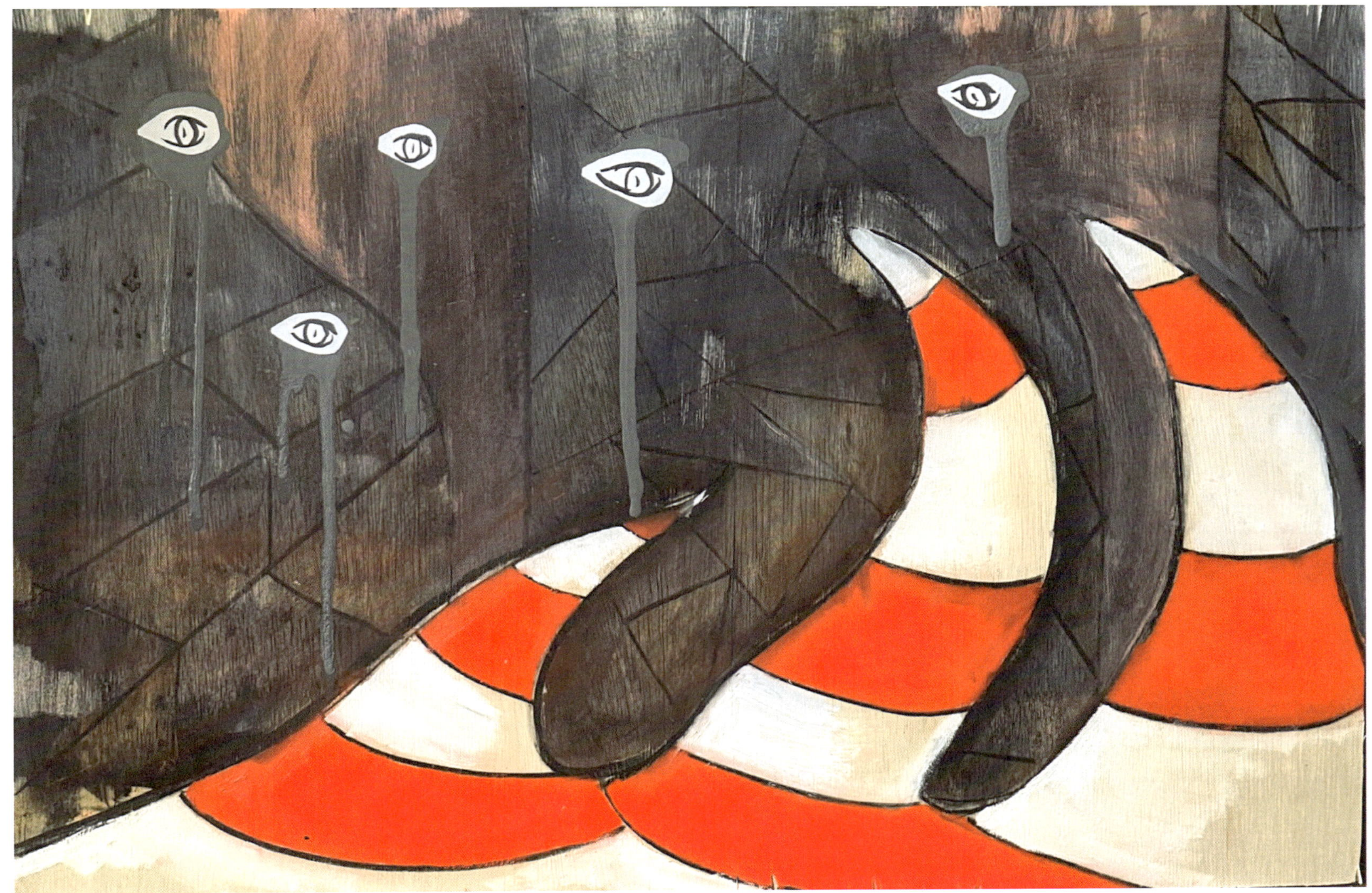

Tentacleese

Oil, acrosol, charcoal, on wood
panel
16"x24"
2023

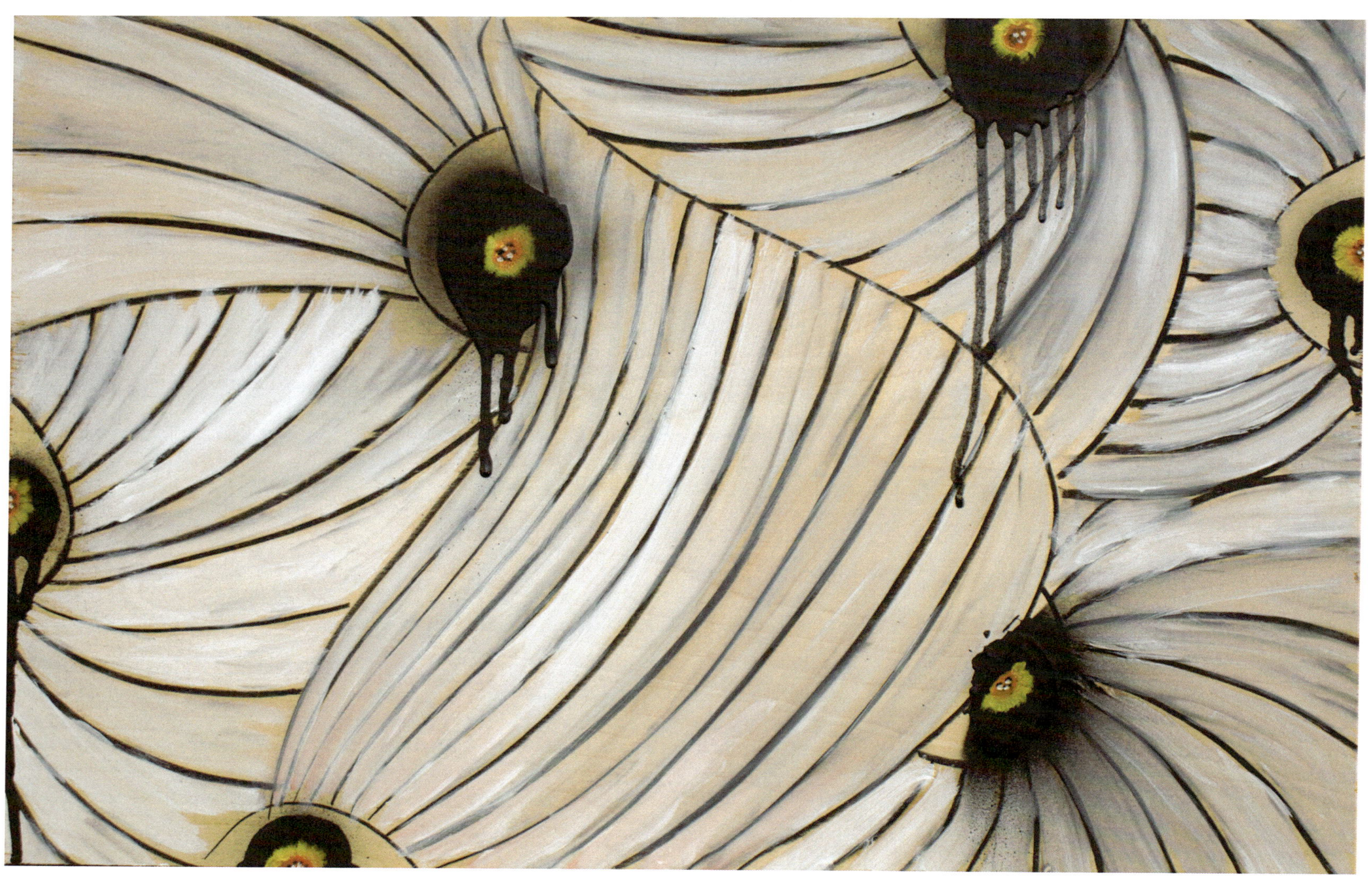

Keno

Oil, aerosol, charcoal, on wood
panel
16"x24"
2023

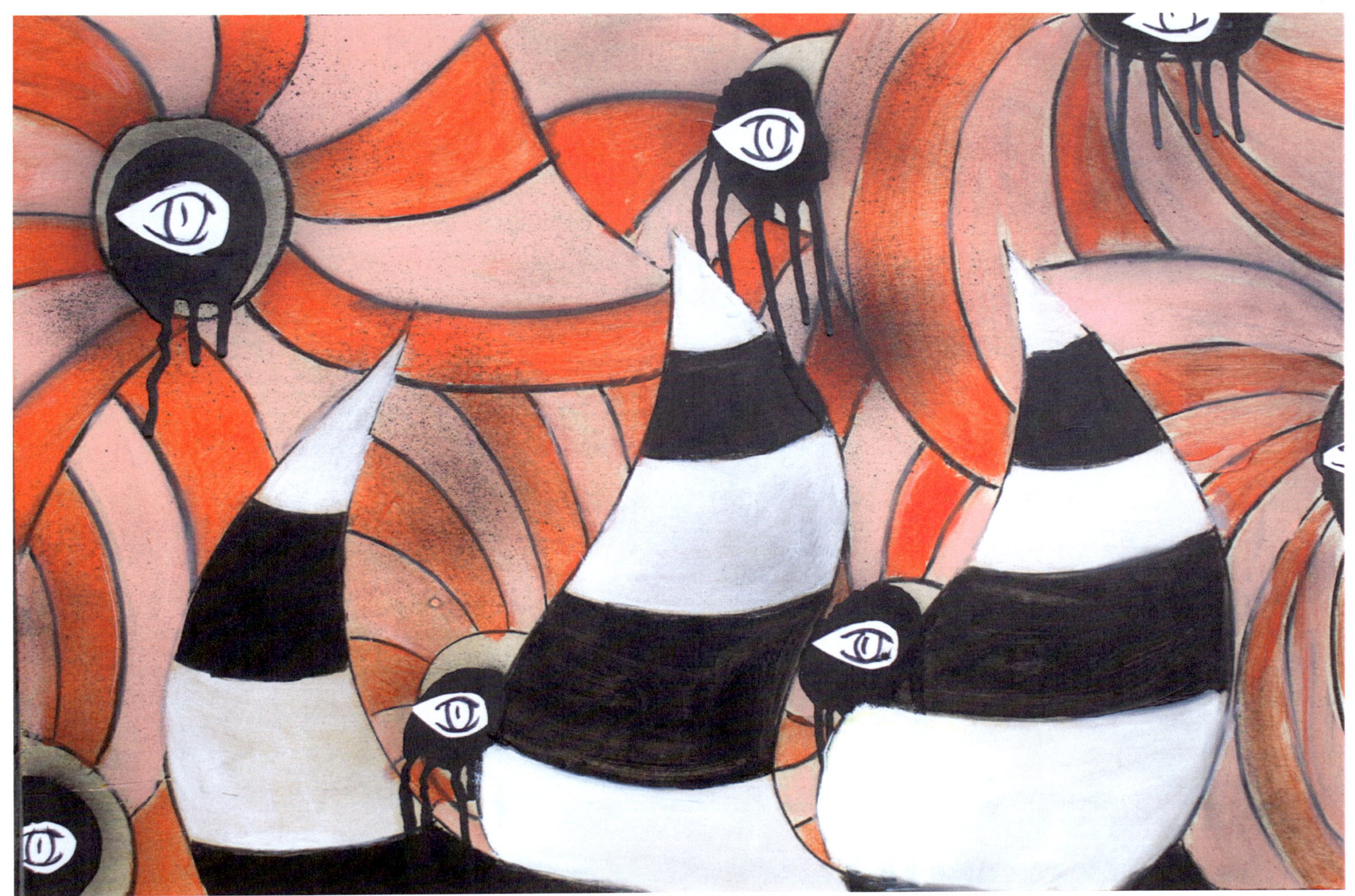

Untitled

Oil, charcoal, aerosol, on wood
panel
16"x24"
2023

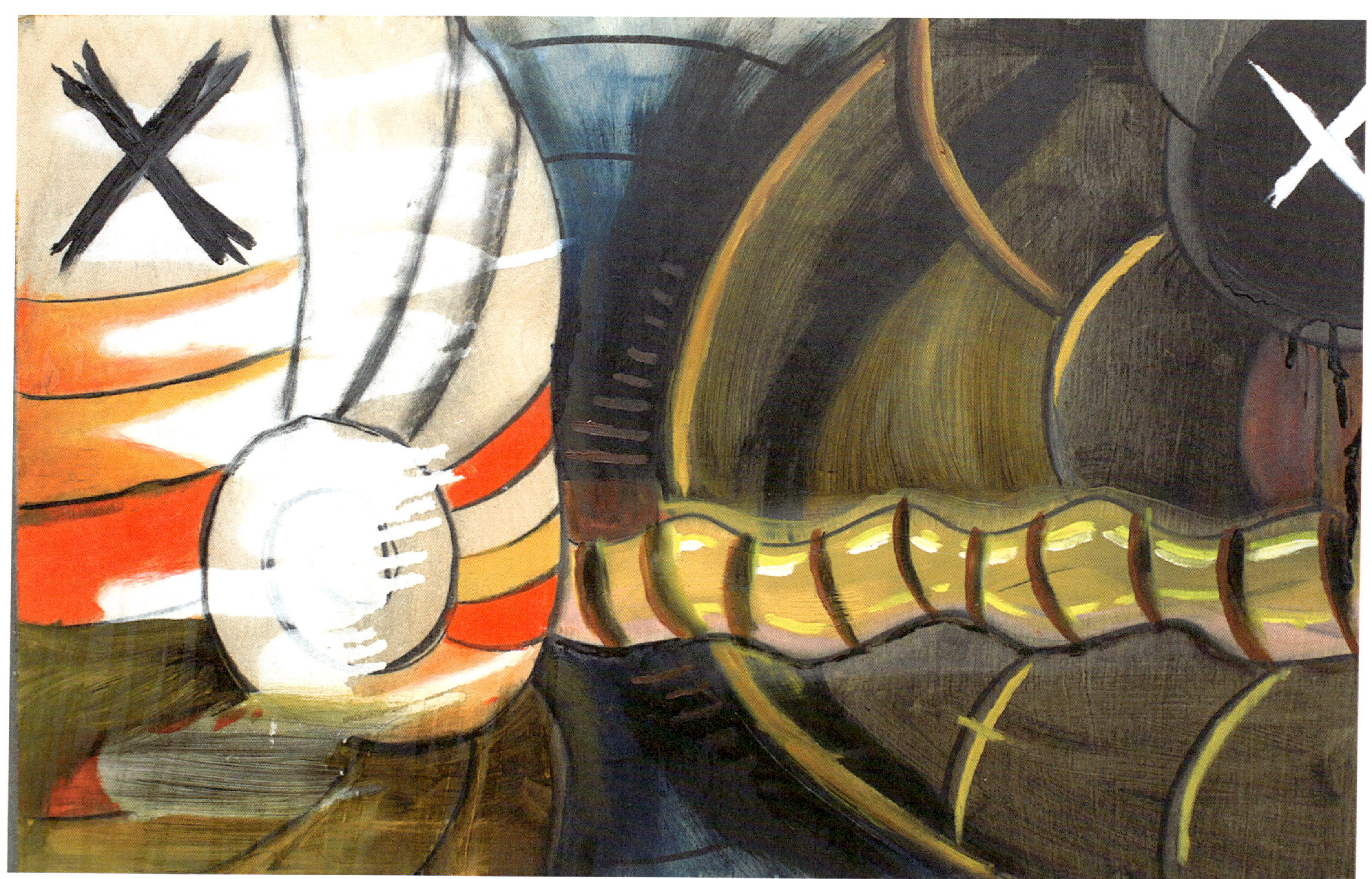

Oksa

Oil, aerosol, graphite, on wood
16"x24"
2023

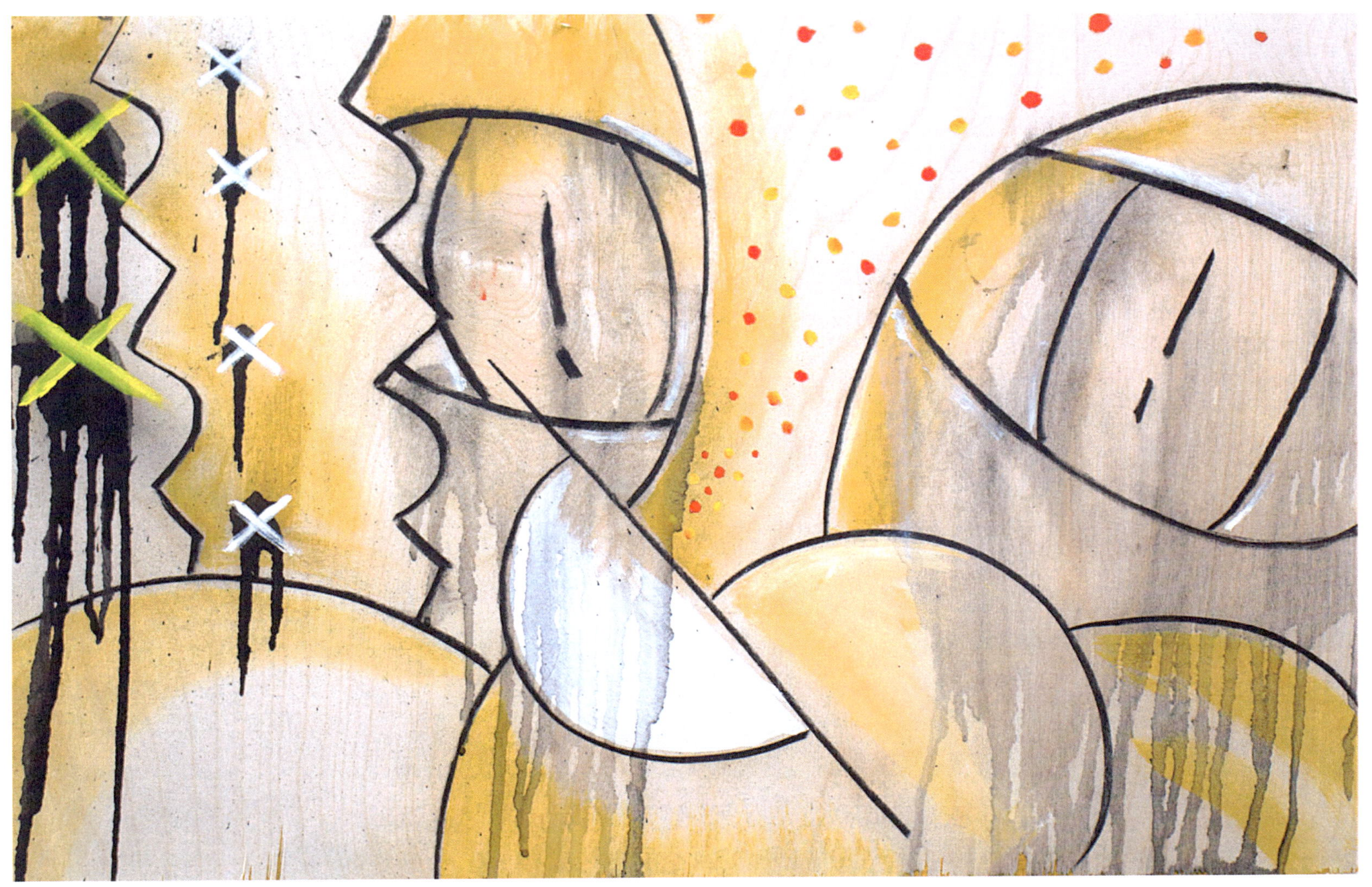

Elavator

Oil, charcoal, aerosol, on wood
panel
16"x24"
2023

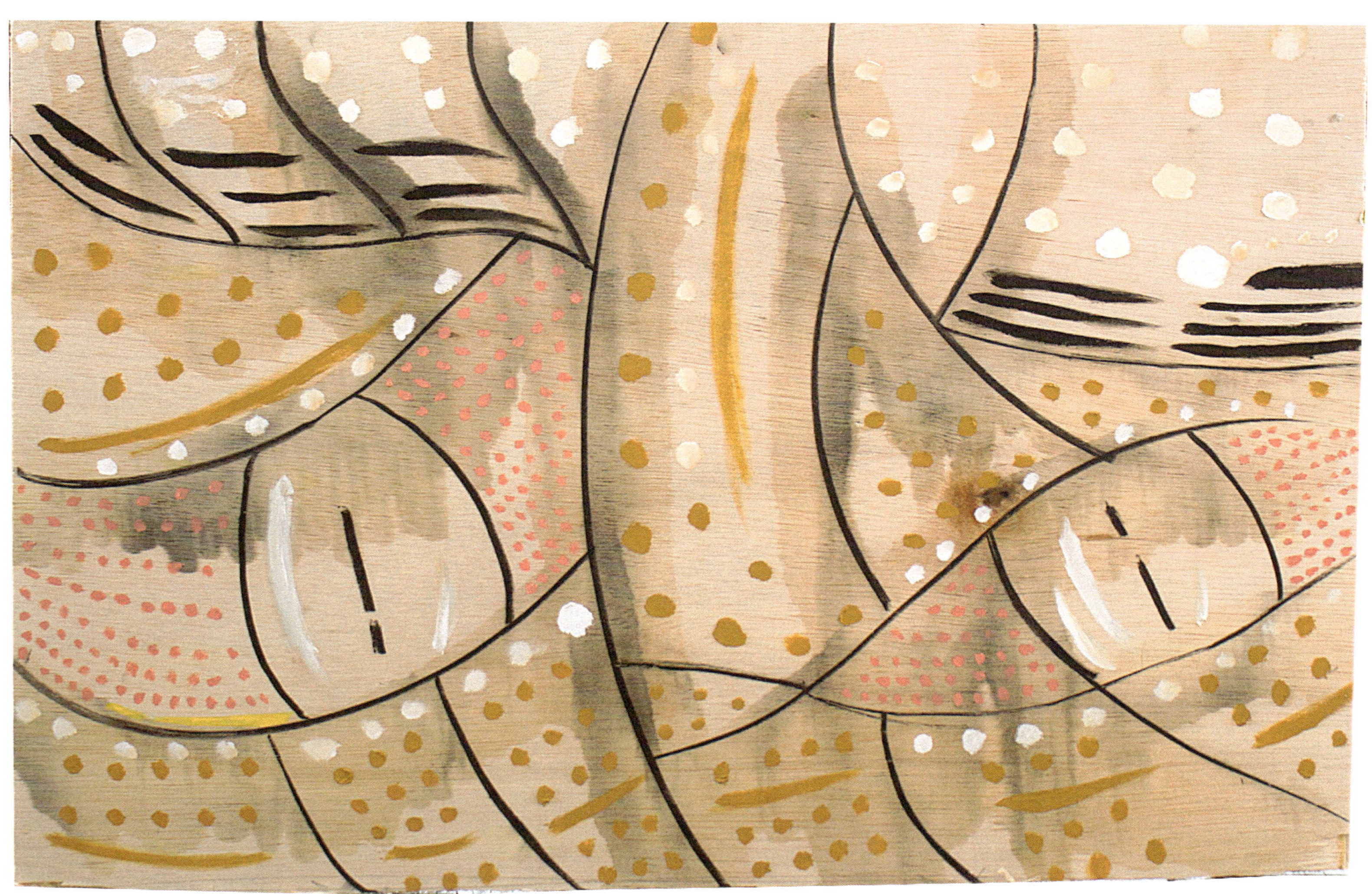

Ellovert

Oil, charcoal, aerosol, on wood panel
16"x24"
2023

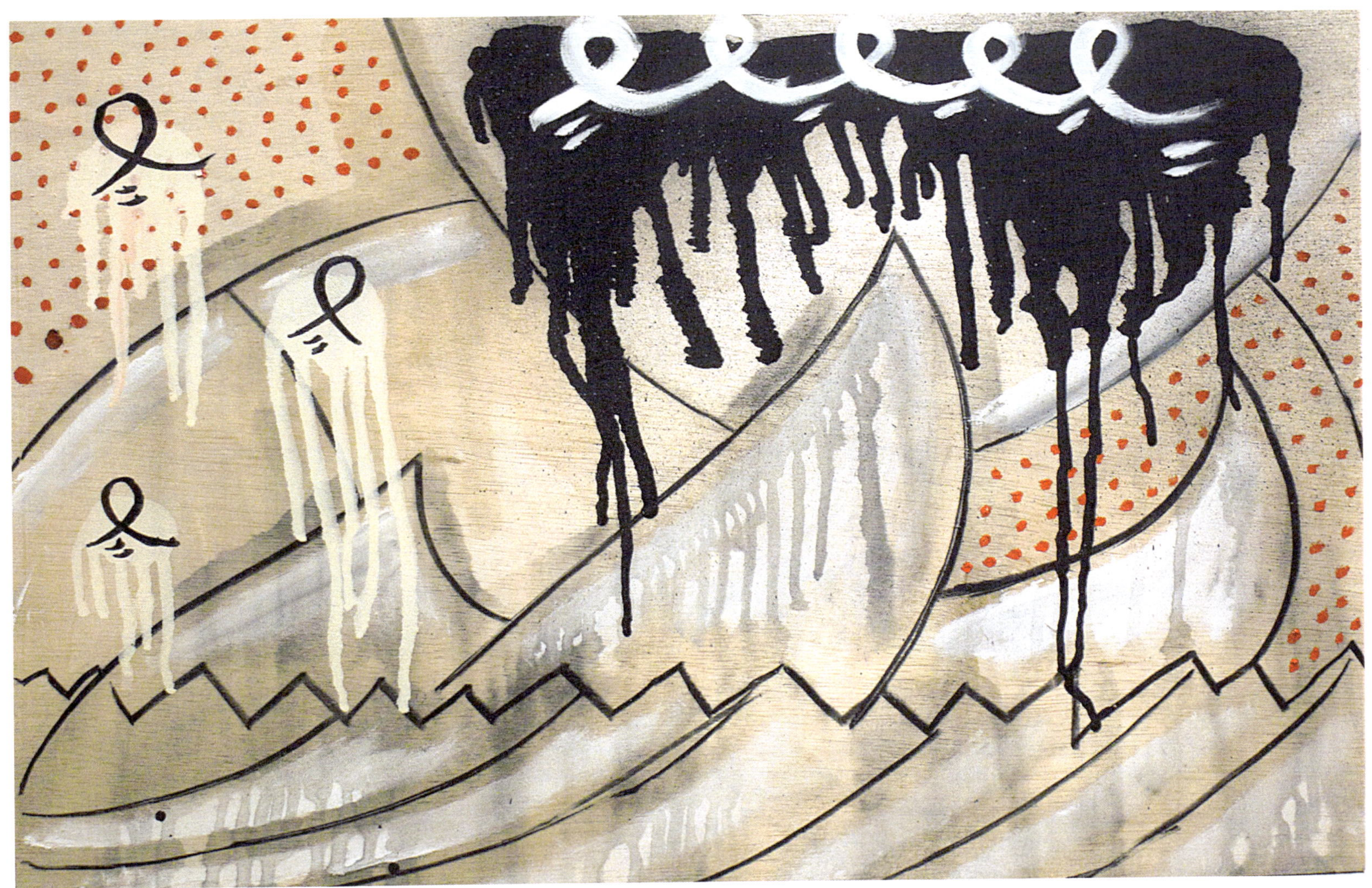

Kedlo

Oil, charcoal, aerosol, ink, on wood
panel
16"x24"
2023

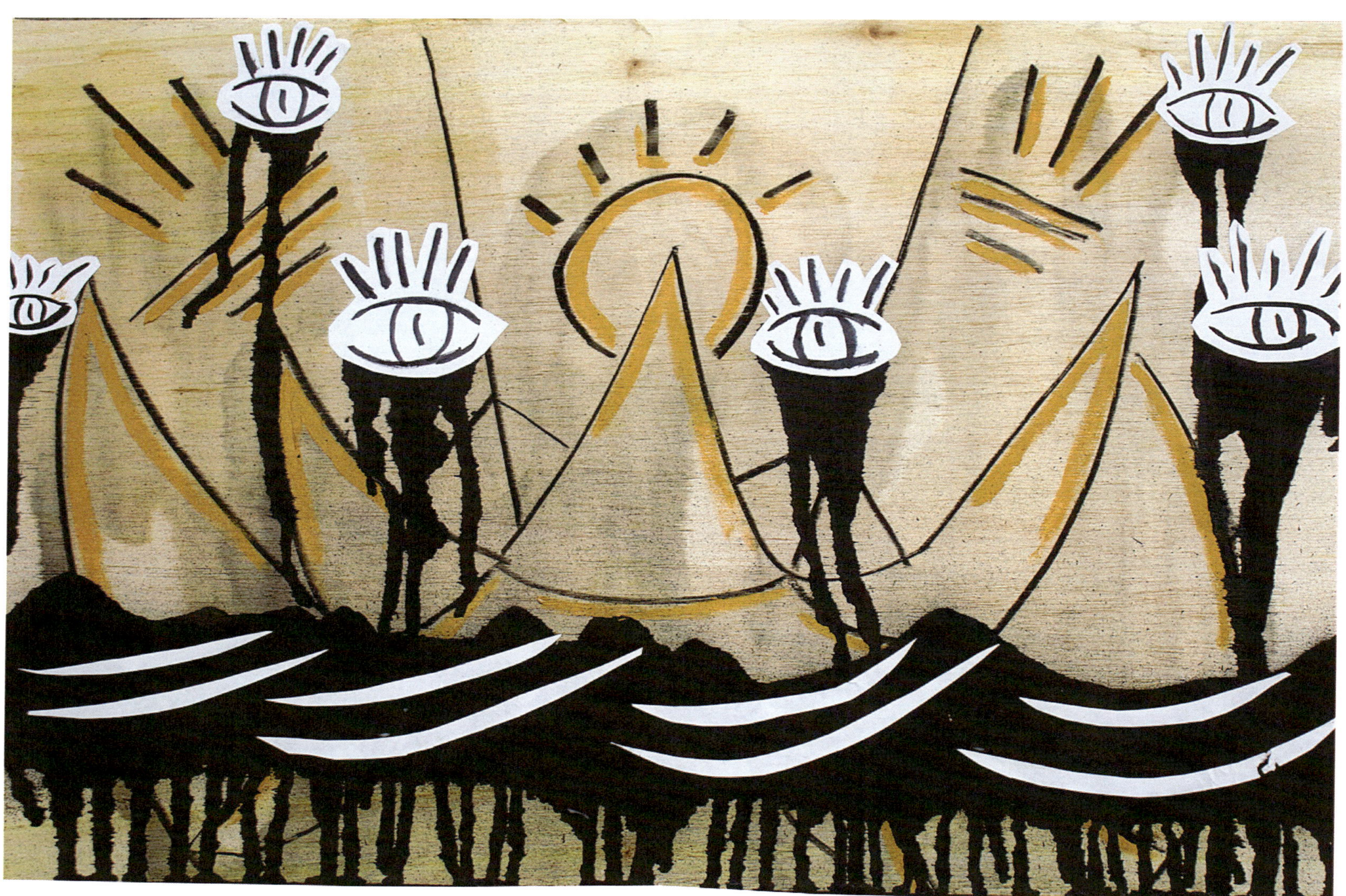

Boyd

Oil, paper, ink, aerosol, charcoal, on
wood
16"x24"
2023

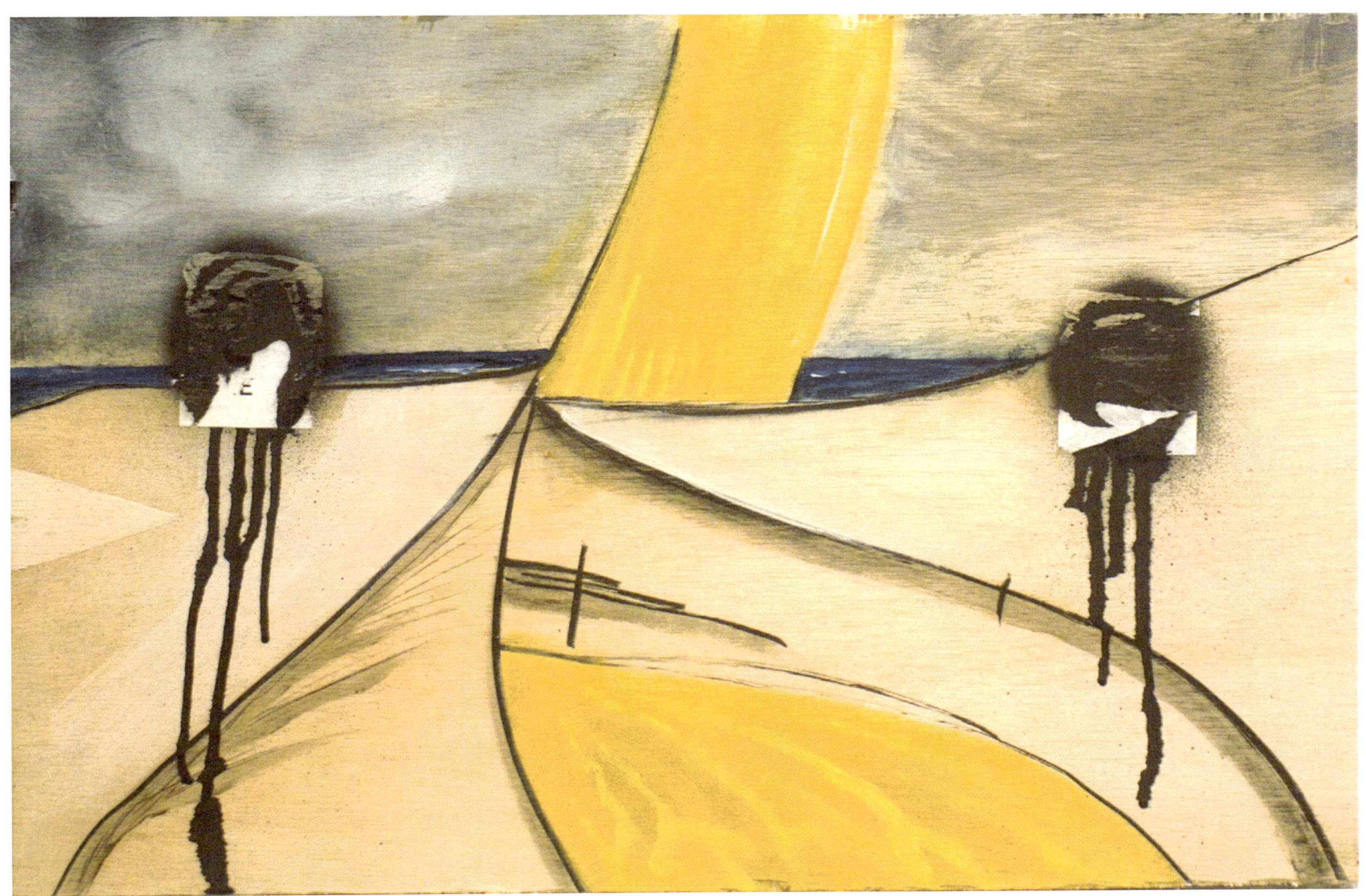

a process of reconcilliation

Oil, paper, glue, aerosol, graphite,
on wood panel
16"x24"
2023

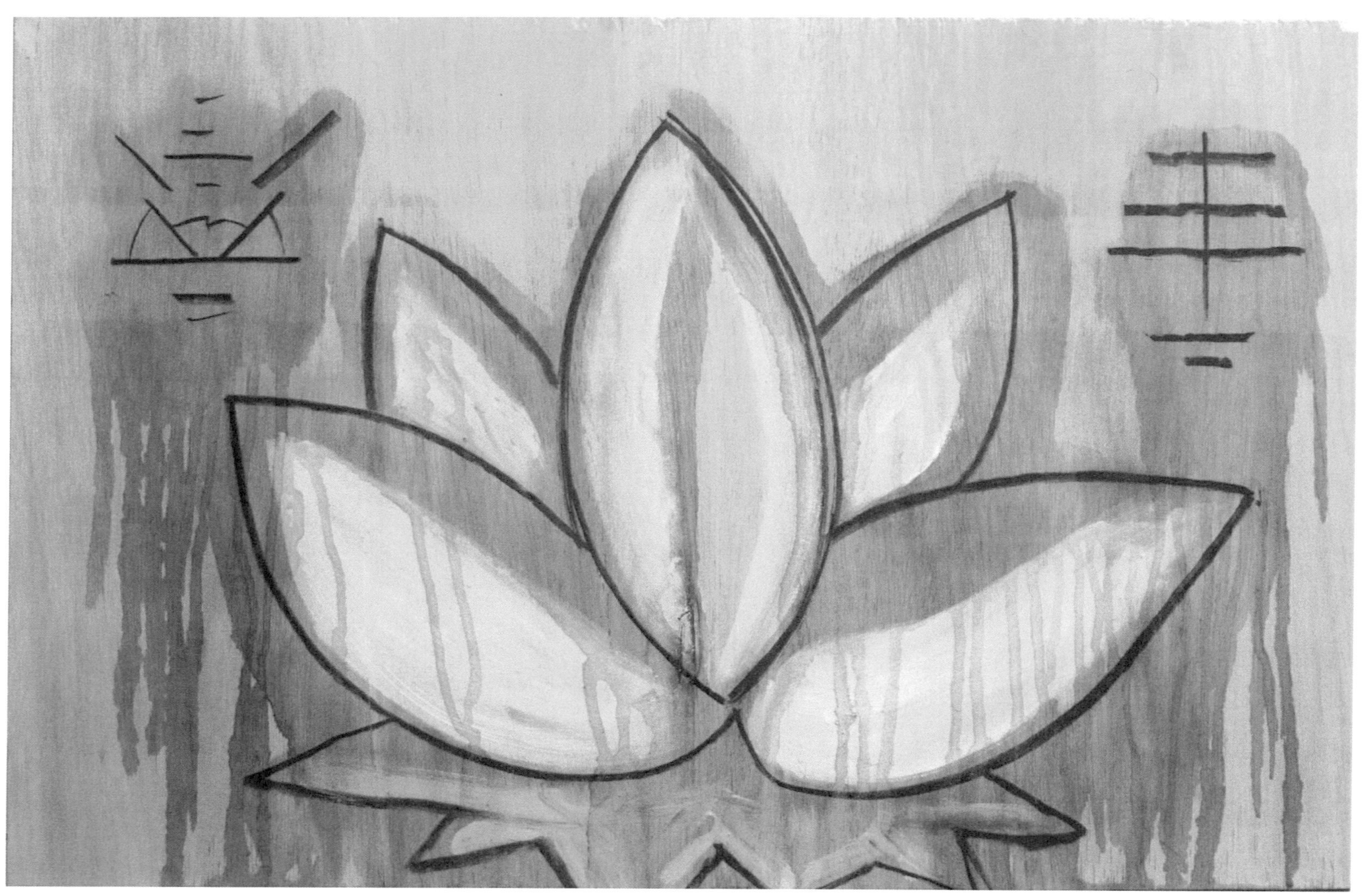

Flower #1

Oil, aerosol, charcoal, on wood
16"x24"
2023

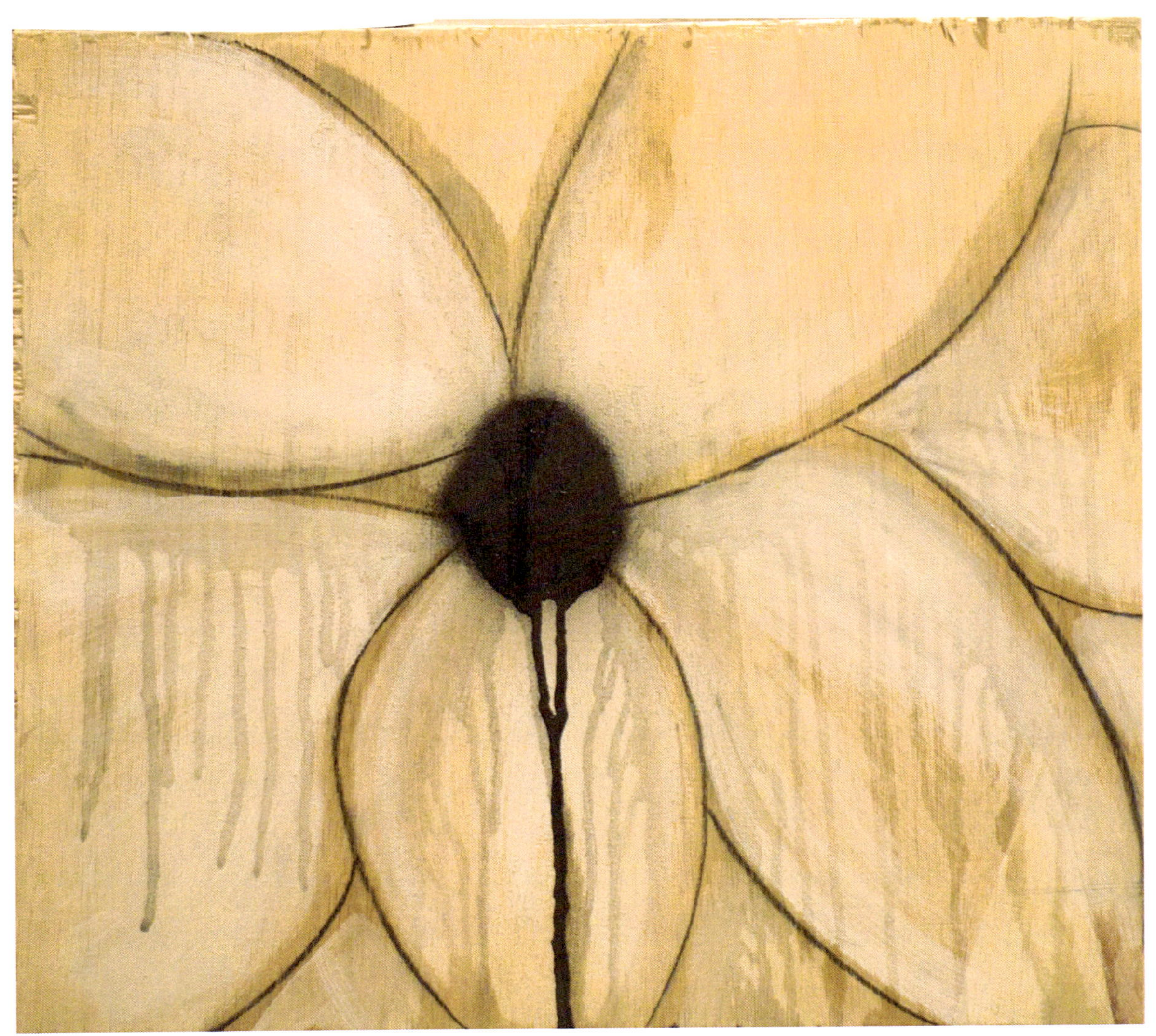

Flower #2

Oil, charcoal, laquer, on wood panel
16"x16"
2024

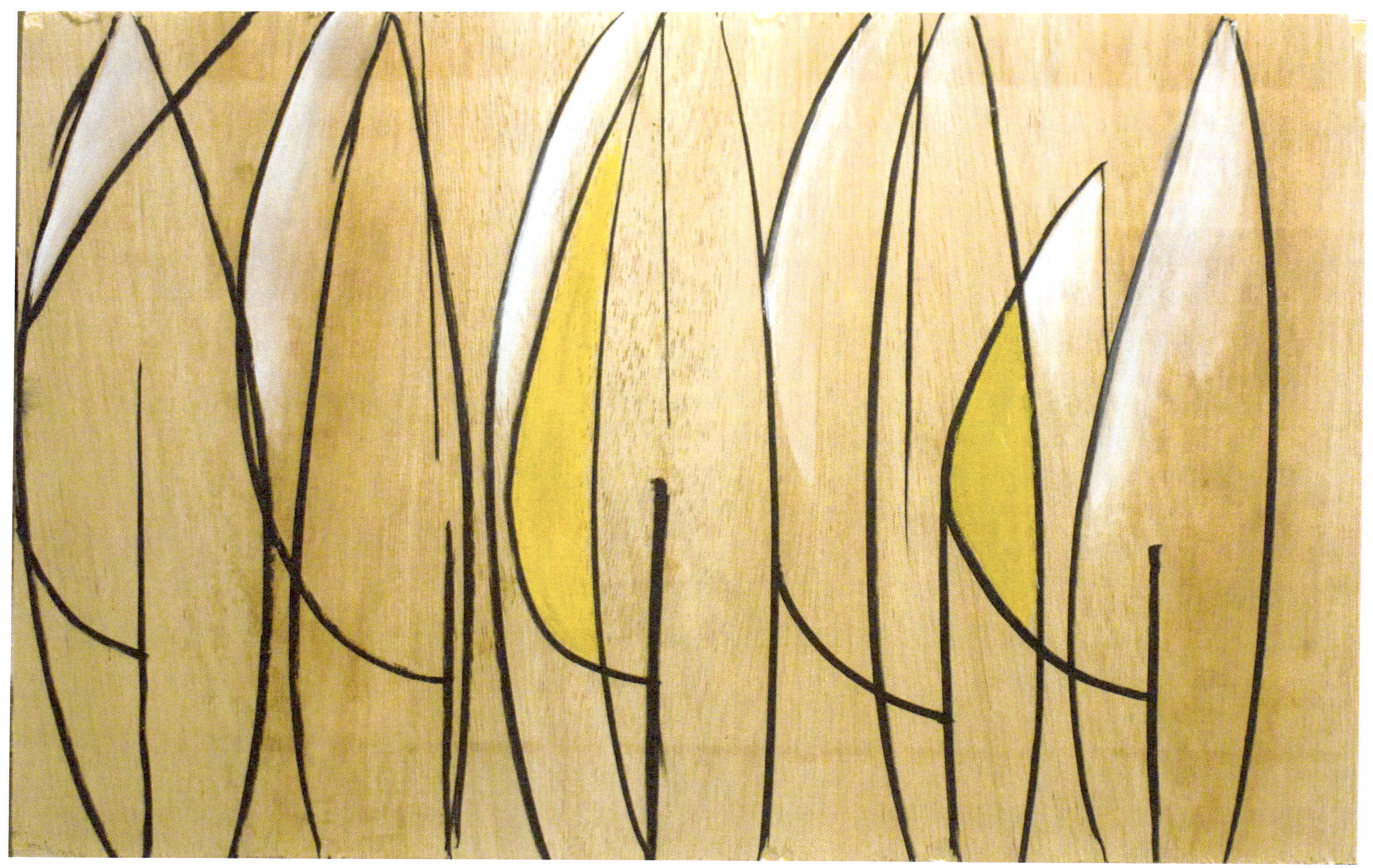

Cloud
Oil, charcoal, on wood panel
16"x24"
2024

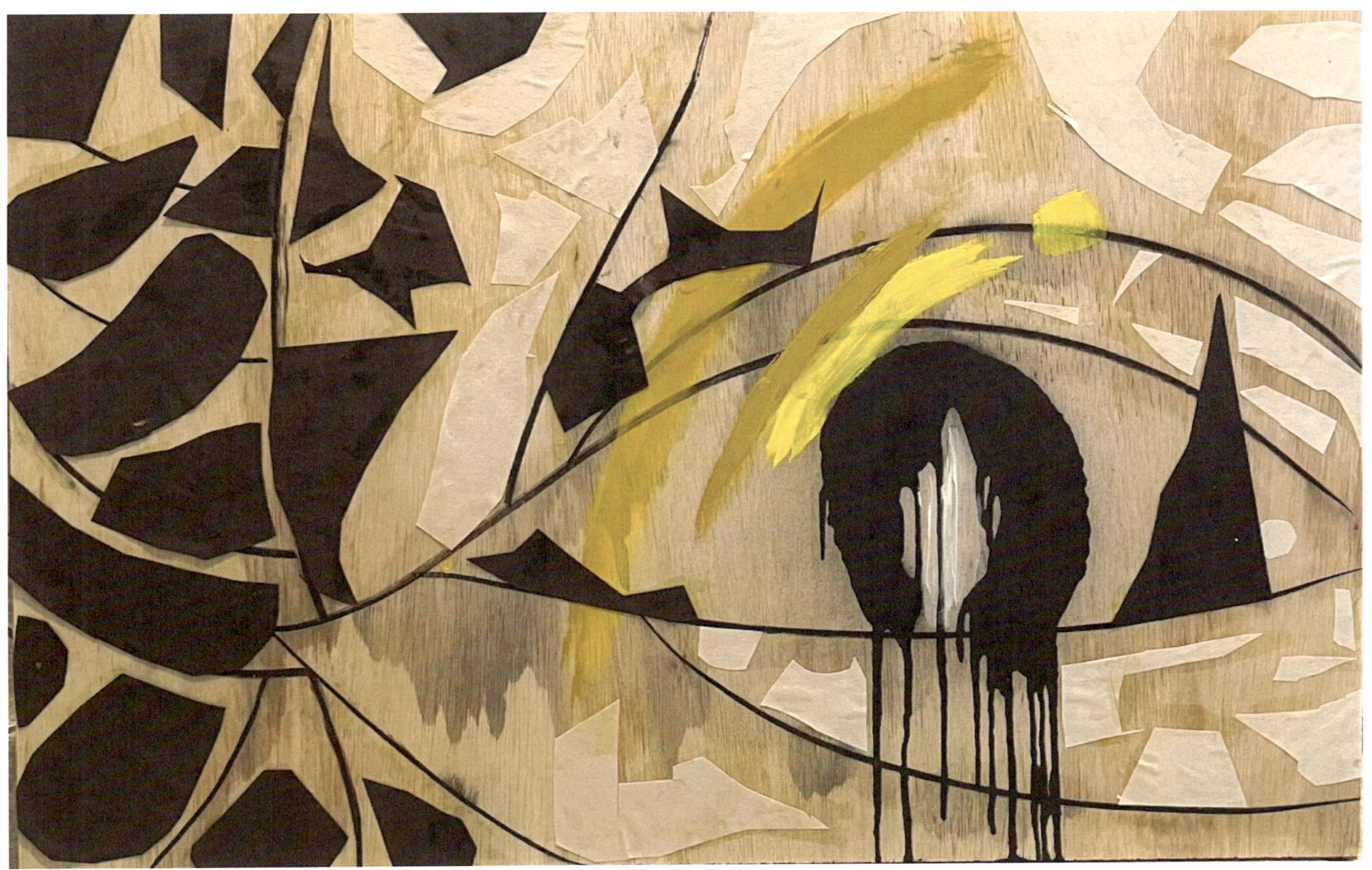

Blue

Oil, paper, aerosol, on wood panel
16"x24"
2024

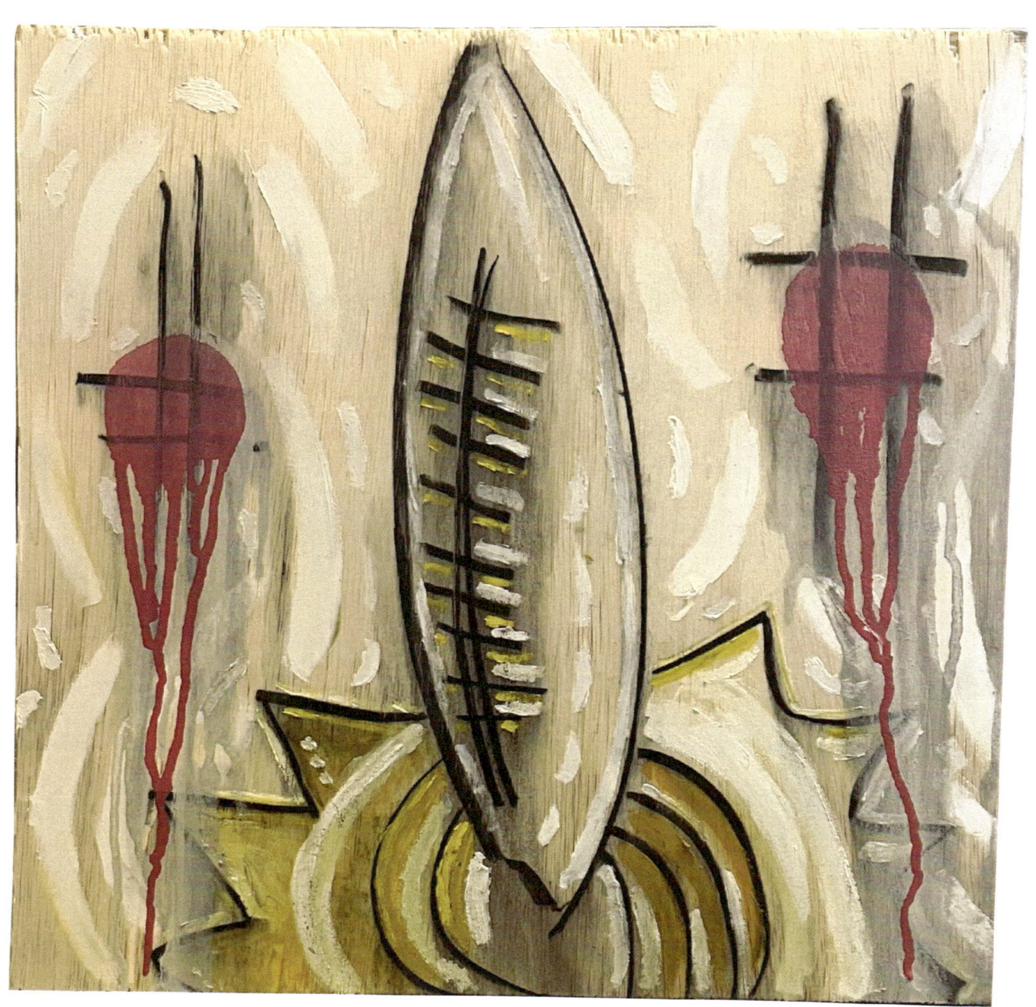

Flower / Feather

Oil, charcoal, aerosol, laquer, on
wood panel
16"x16"
2024

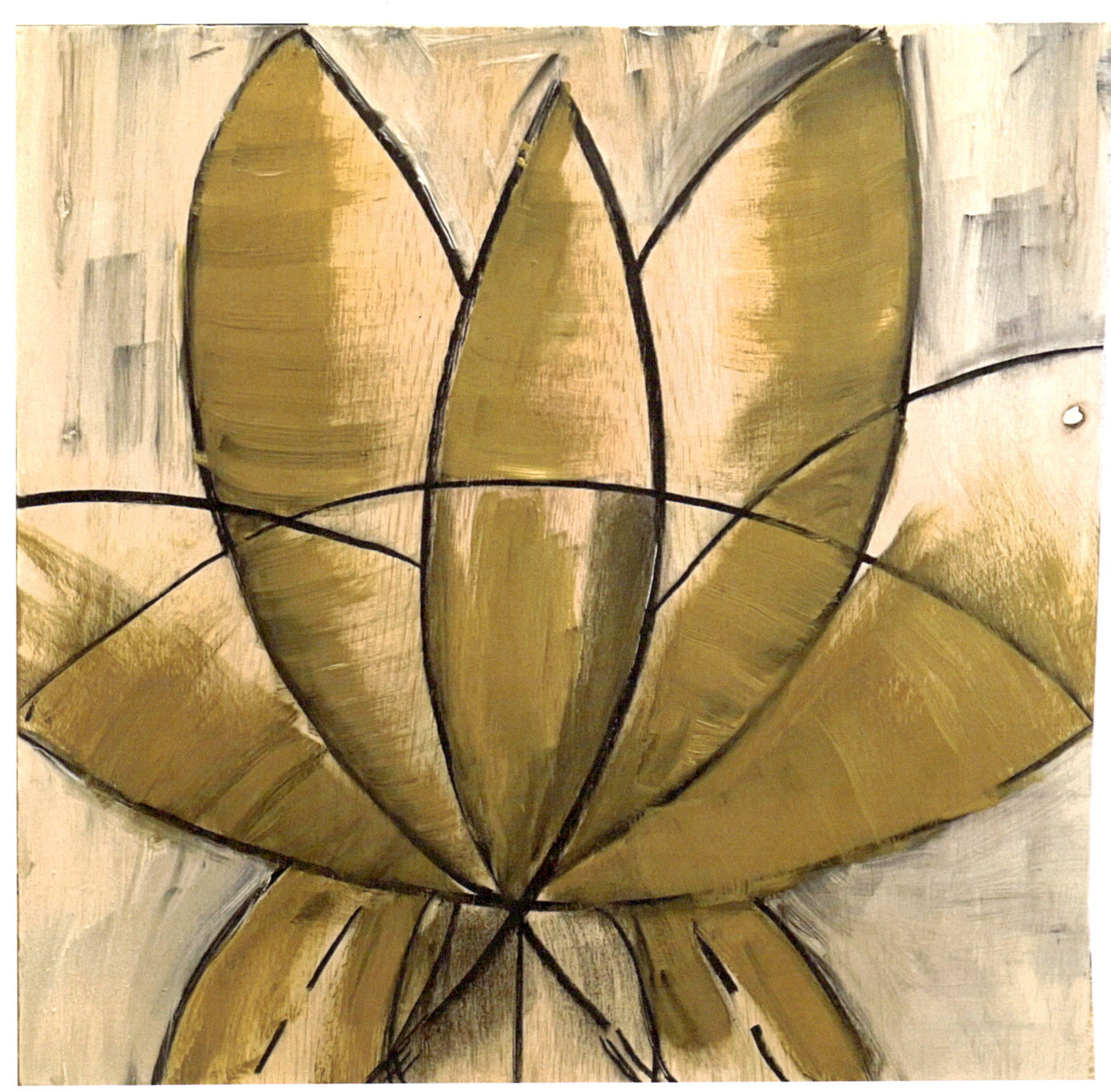

Goldenflower

Oil, charcoal, on wood panel
16"x16"
2024

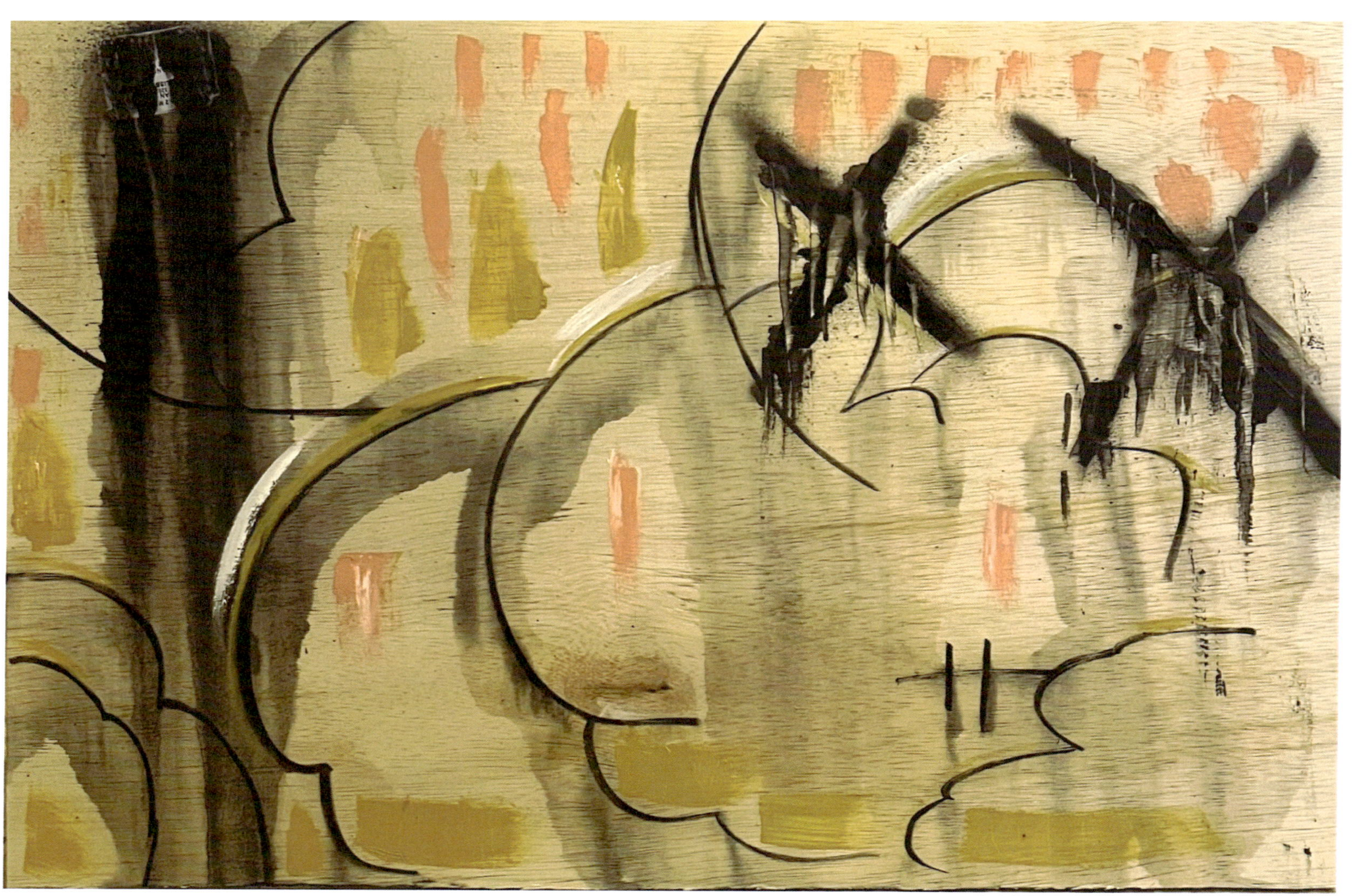

Arah

Oil, charcoal, aerosol, on wood panel
16"x24"
2024

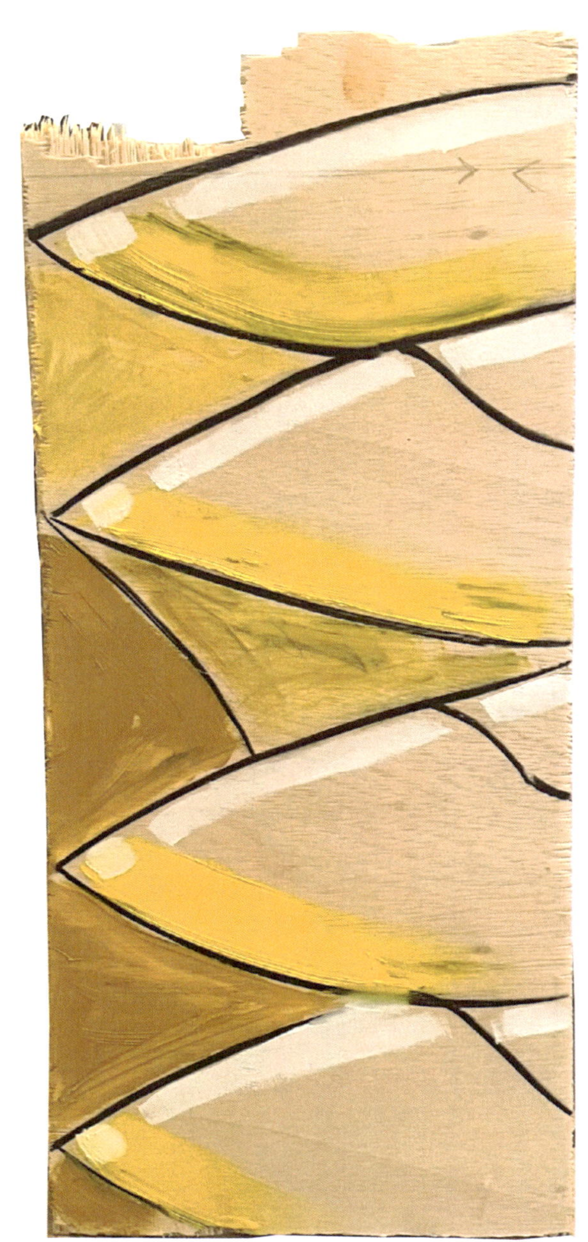

Bells

Oil, charcoal, on wood panel
8"x16"
2024

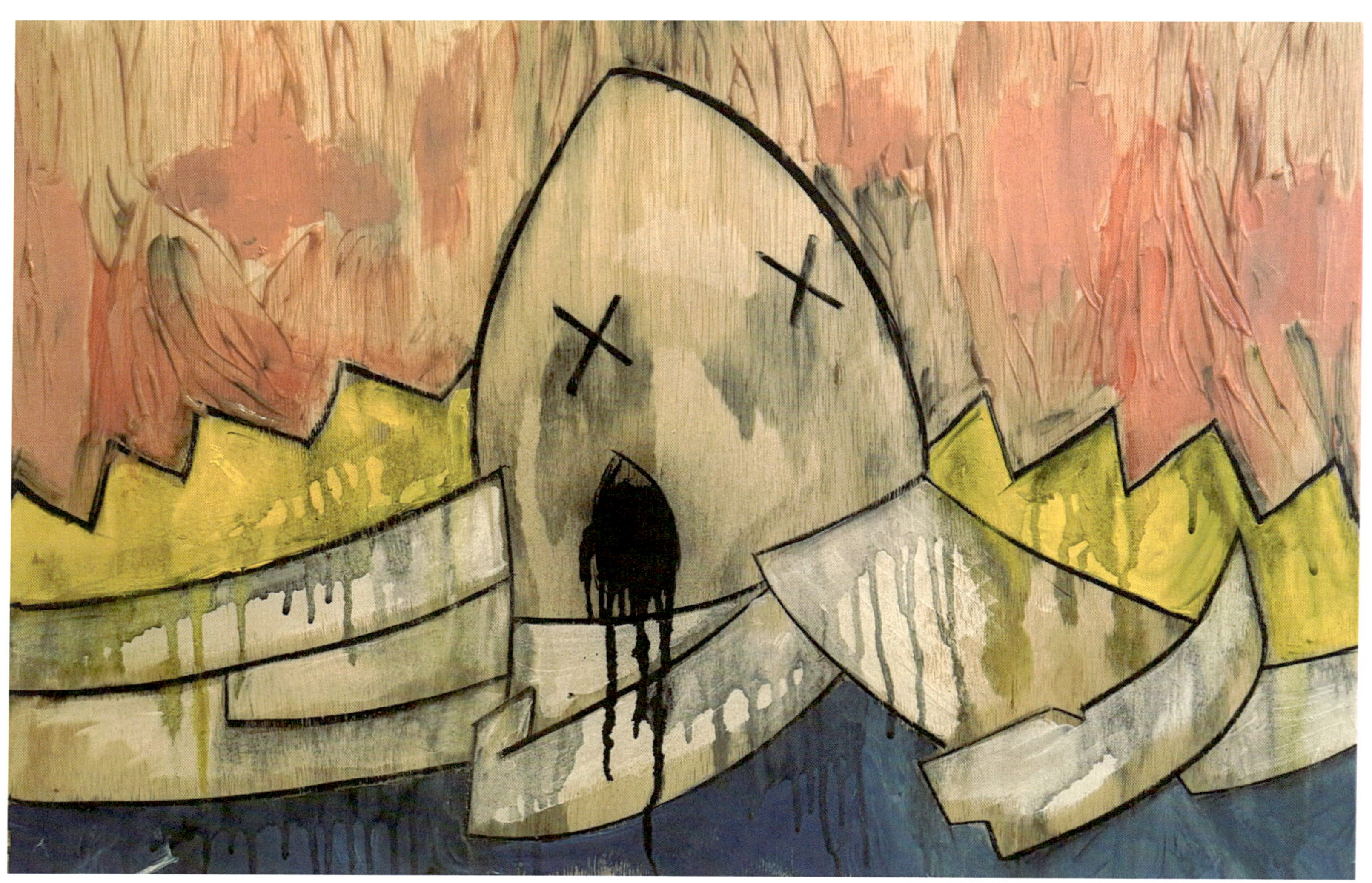

Boatbreaker

Oil, medium, charcoal, aerosol,
laquer, on wood panel
16"x24"
2024

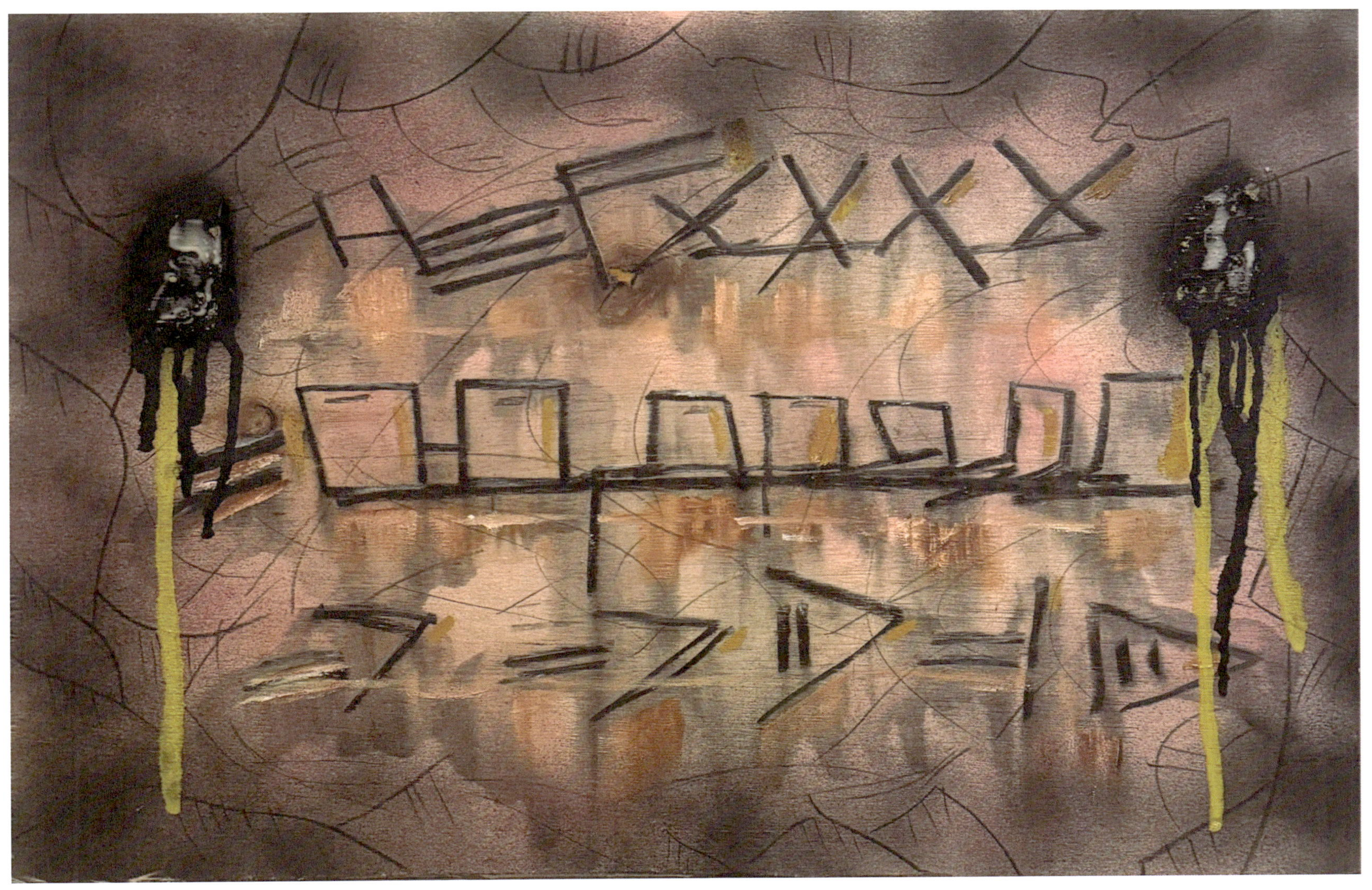

D2

Oil, charcoal, aerosol, adhesive,
laquer, on wood panel
16"x24"
2024

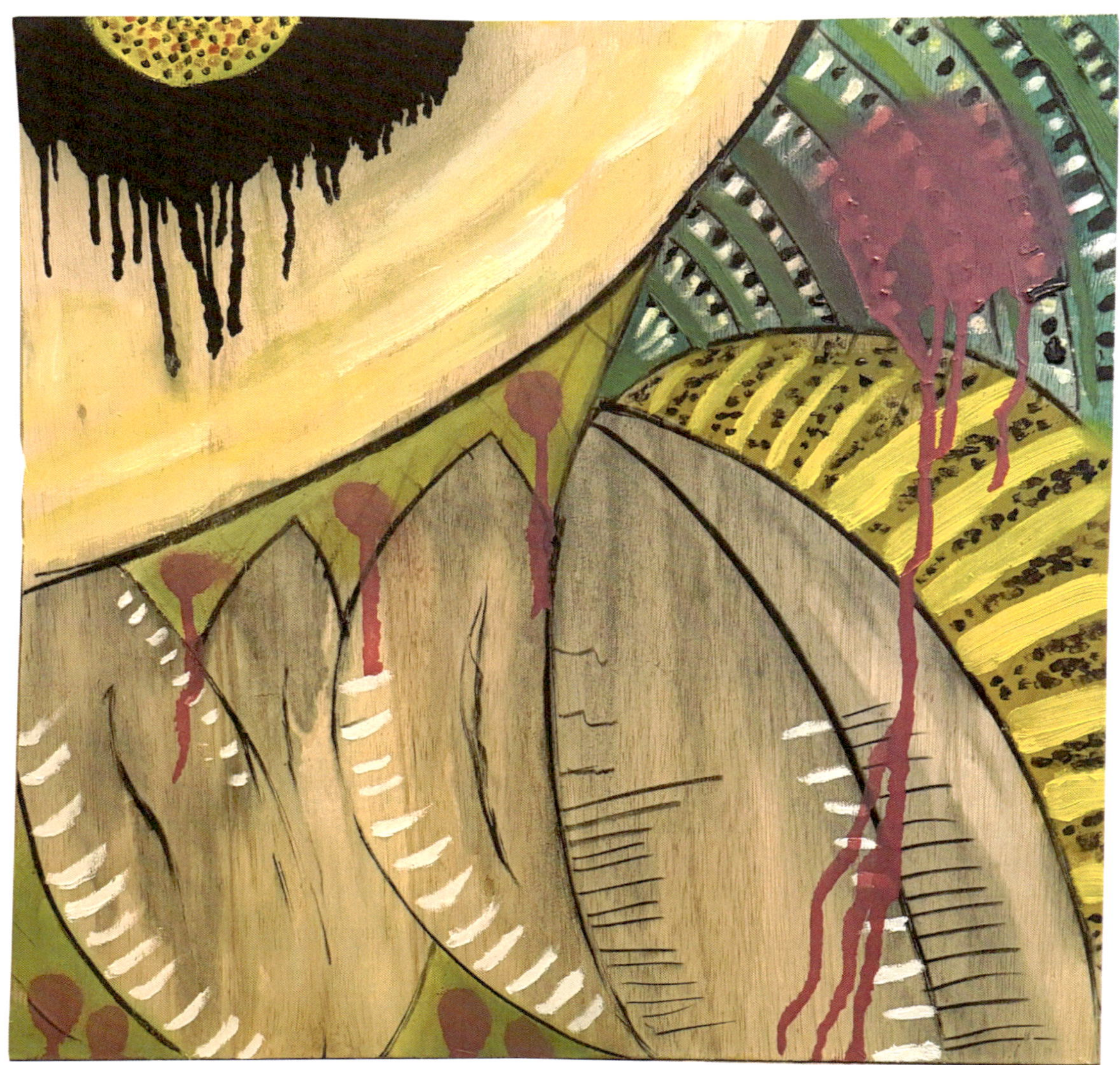

Flowerer

Oil, charcoal, laquer, aerosol, on wood panel
16"x16"
2024

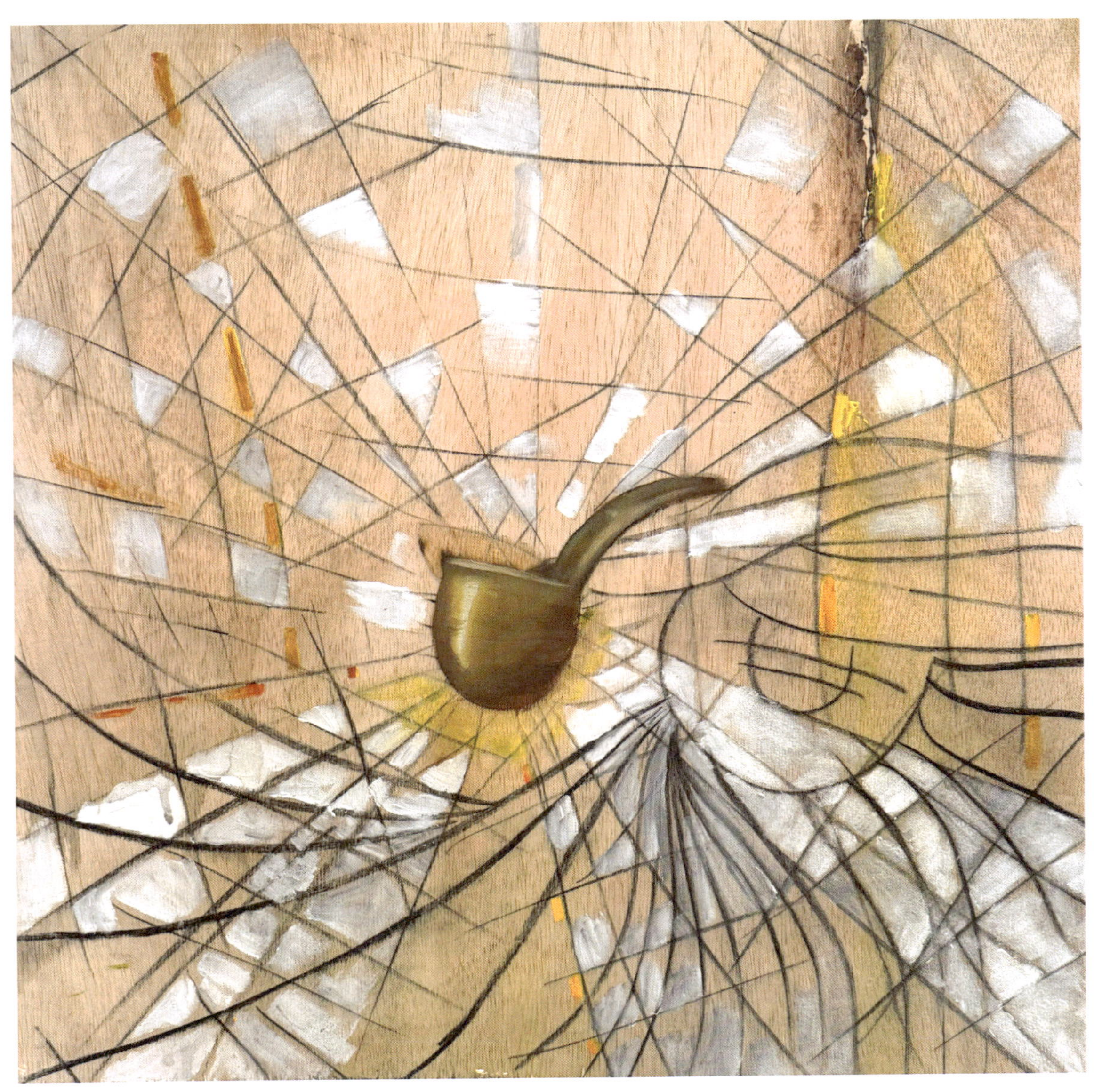

Pipe?

Oil, charcoal, aerosol, on wood
panel
16"x16"
2024

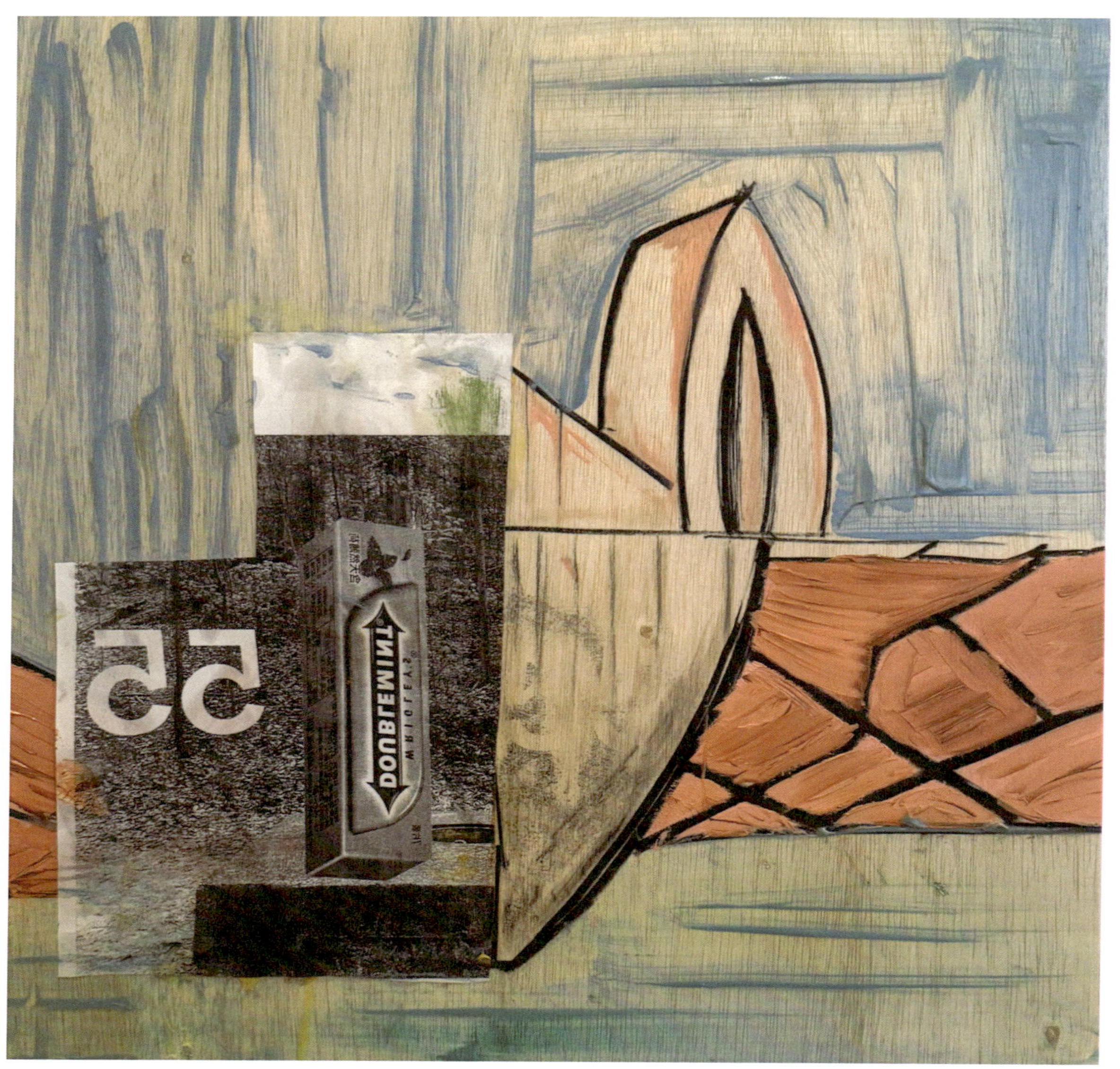

Untitledr

Oil, thermal print, charcoal, laquer,
on wood panel
16"x16"
2024

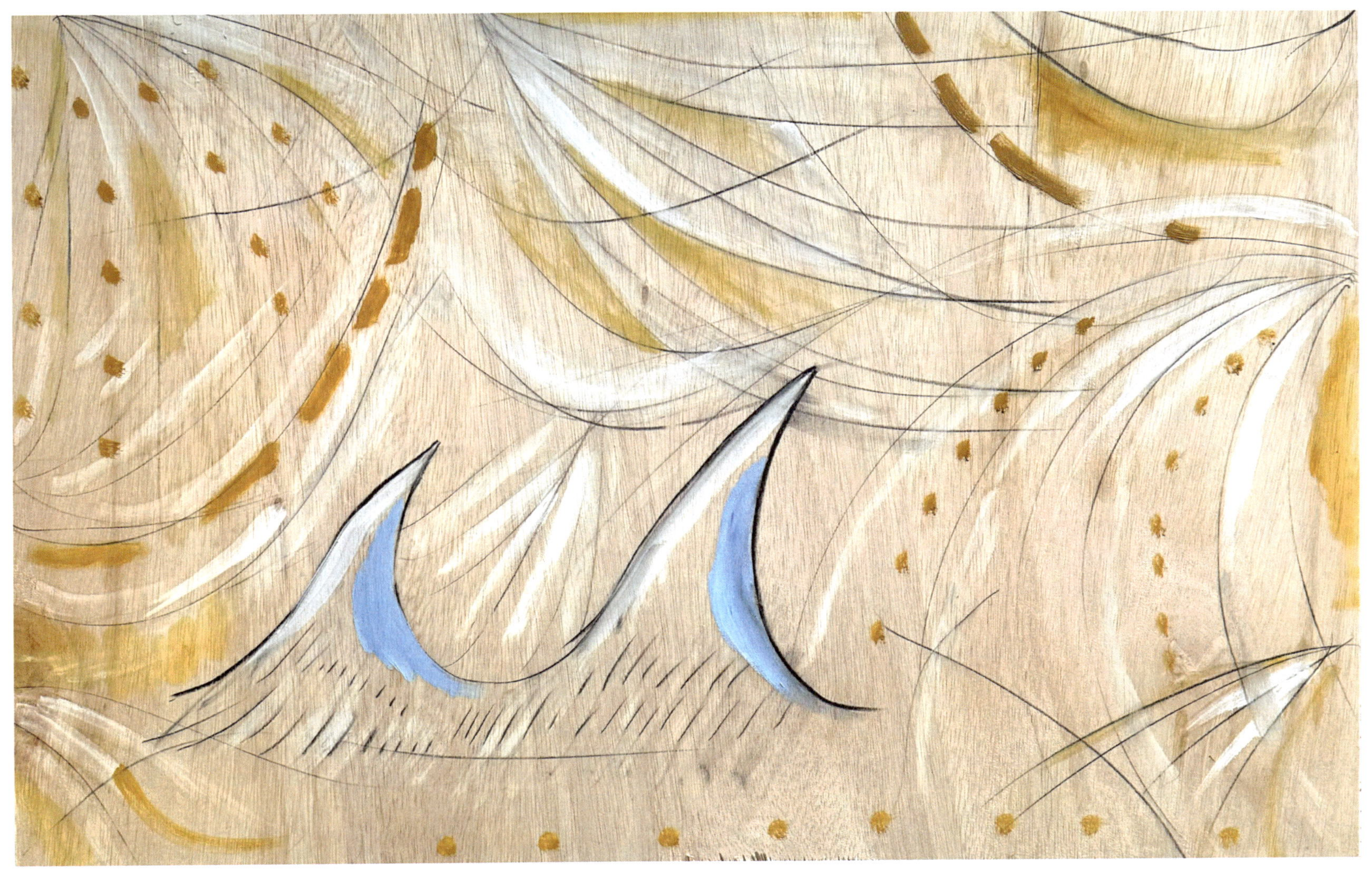

Wavr

Oil, charcoal, on wood panel
16"x24"
2024

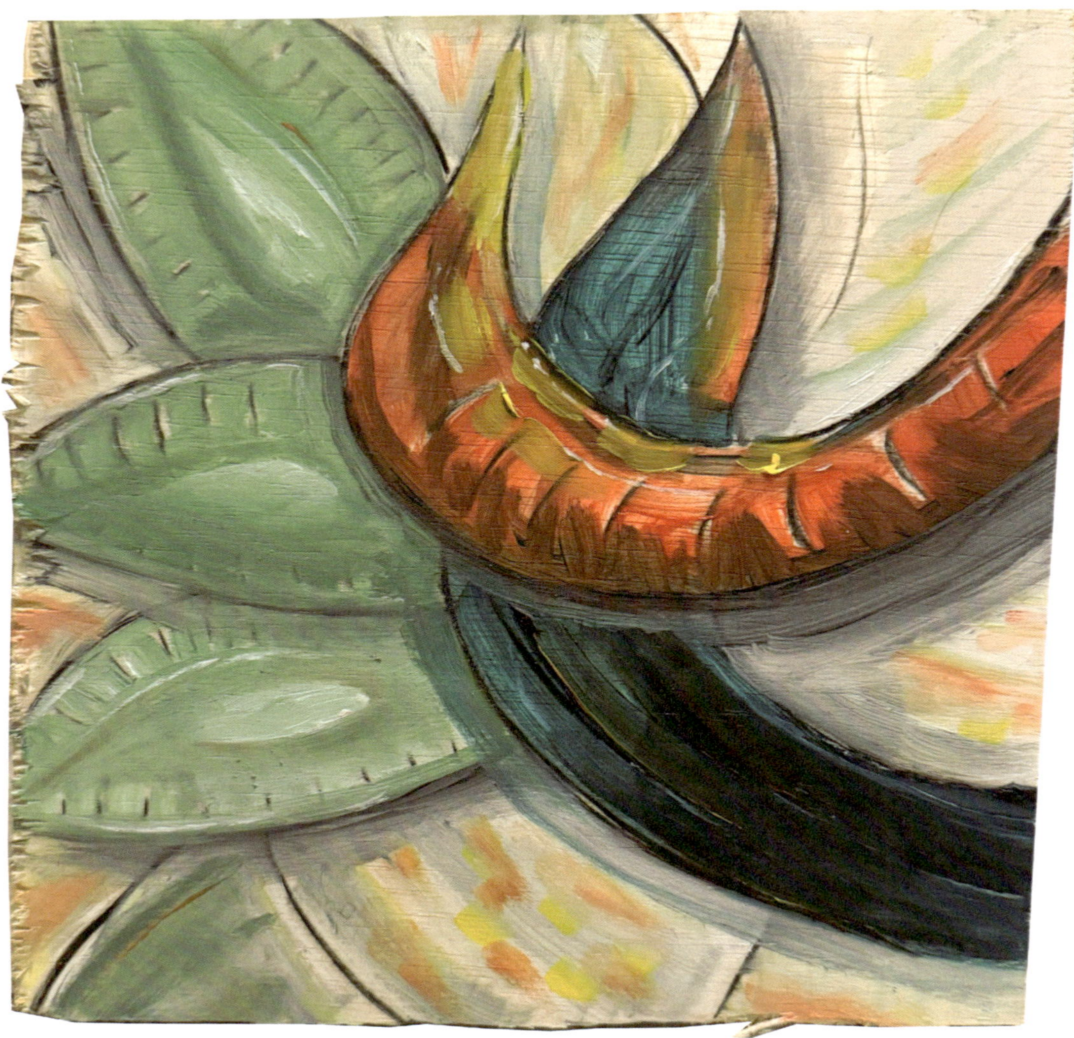

Garden #1

Oil, charcoal, on wood panel
8.25"x8.5"
2024

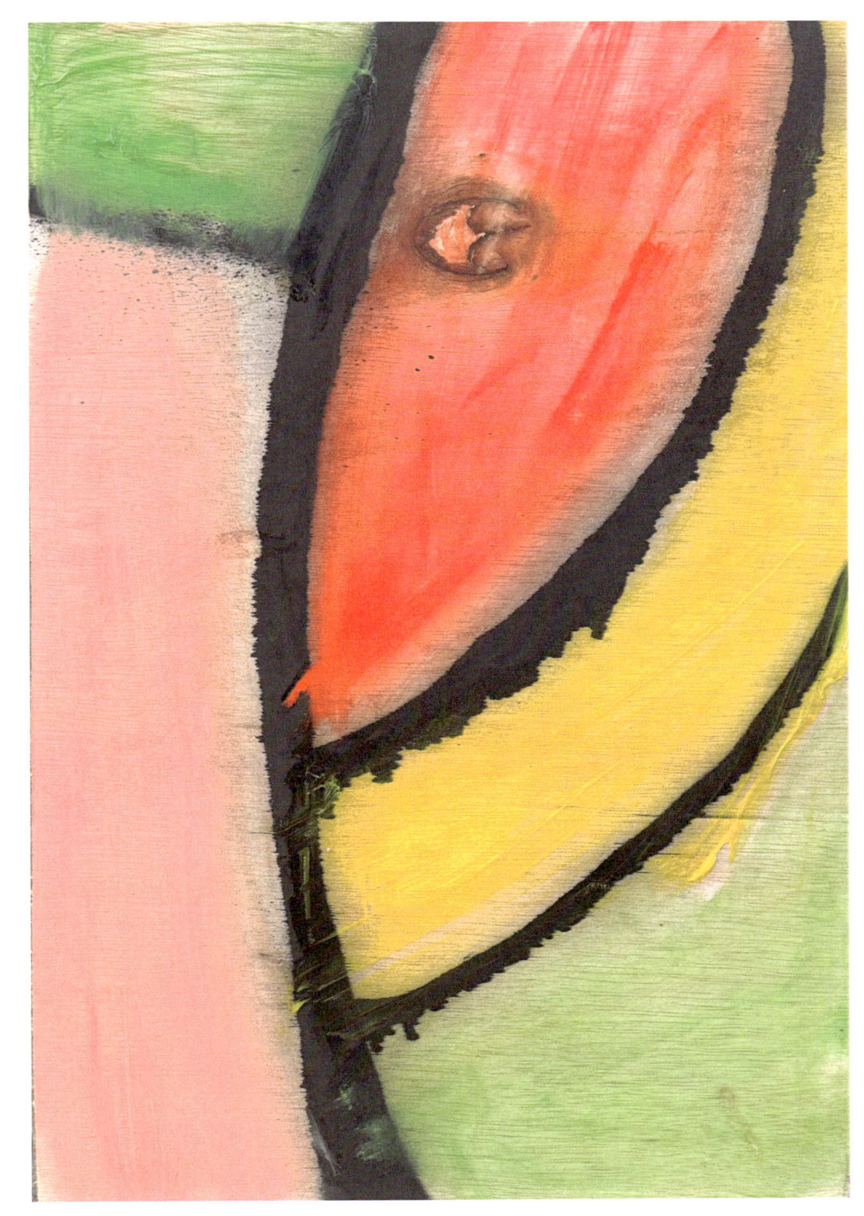

BRRS

Oil, aerosol, on wood panel
16"x24"
2024

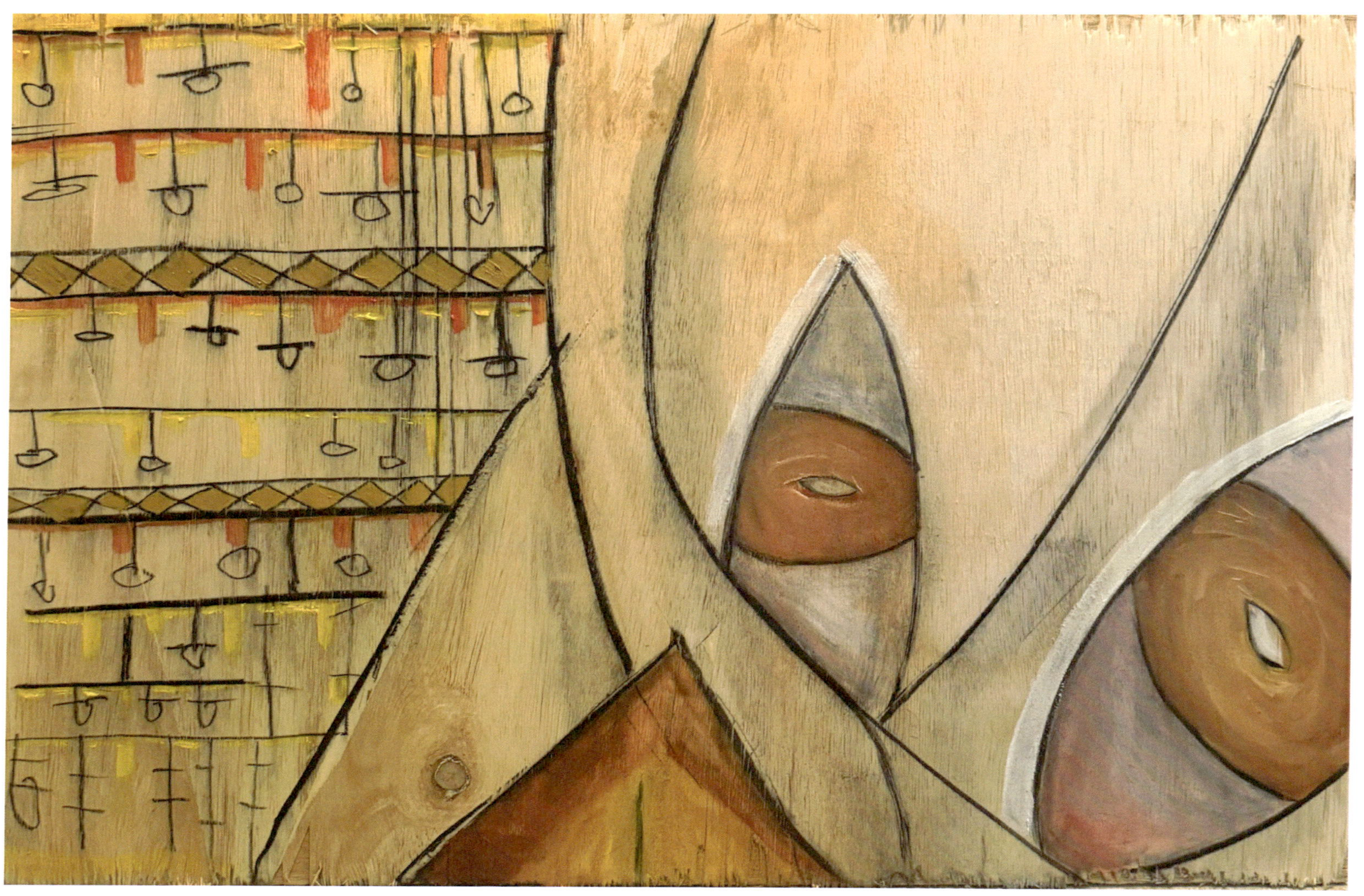

XRRS

Oil, aerosol, laquer, charcoal, on wood panel
16"x24"
2024

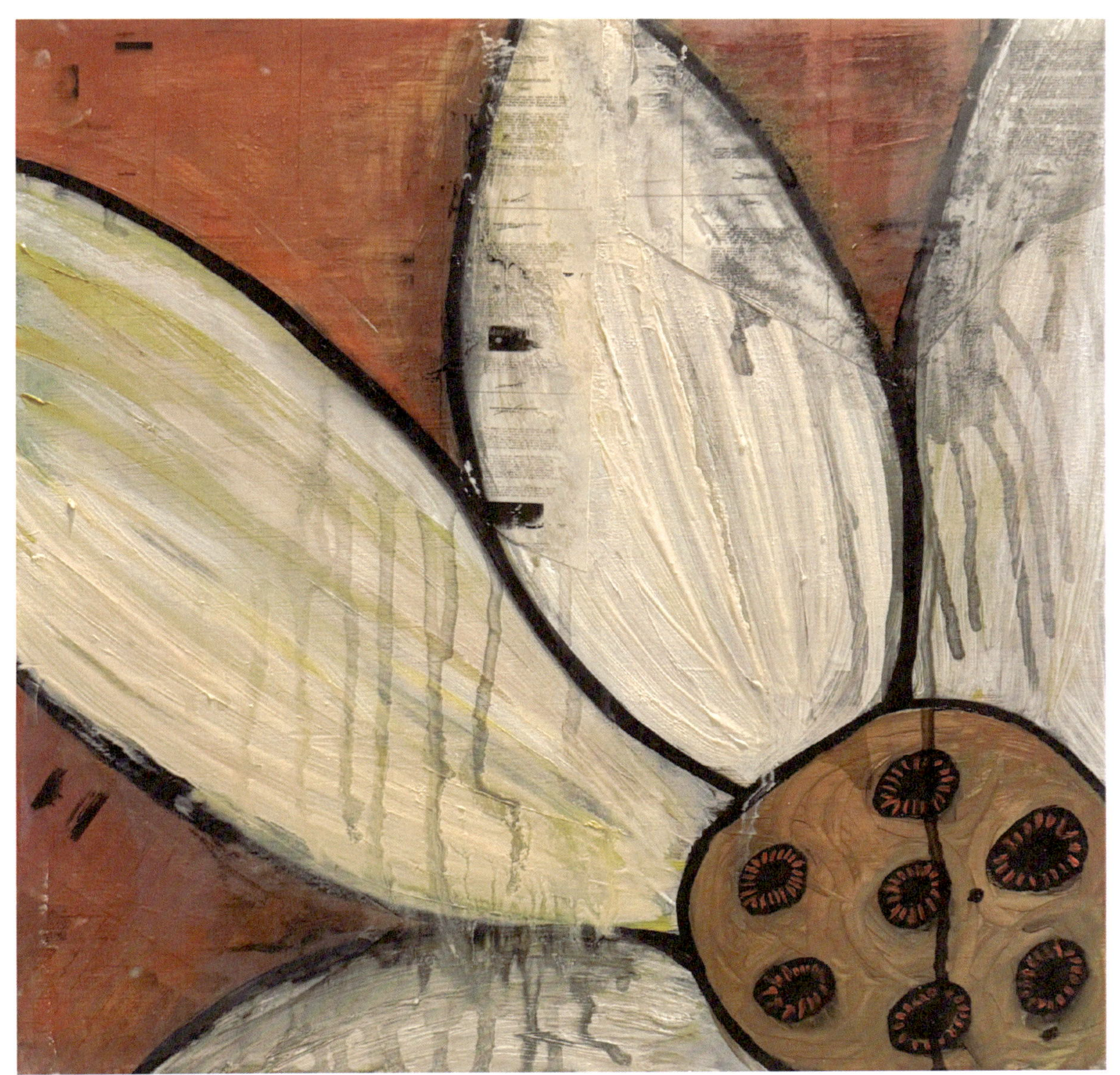

FLWRR

Oil, laquer, thermal print on acetate,
charcoal, on wood panel
16"x16"
2024

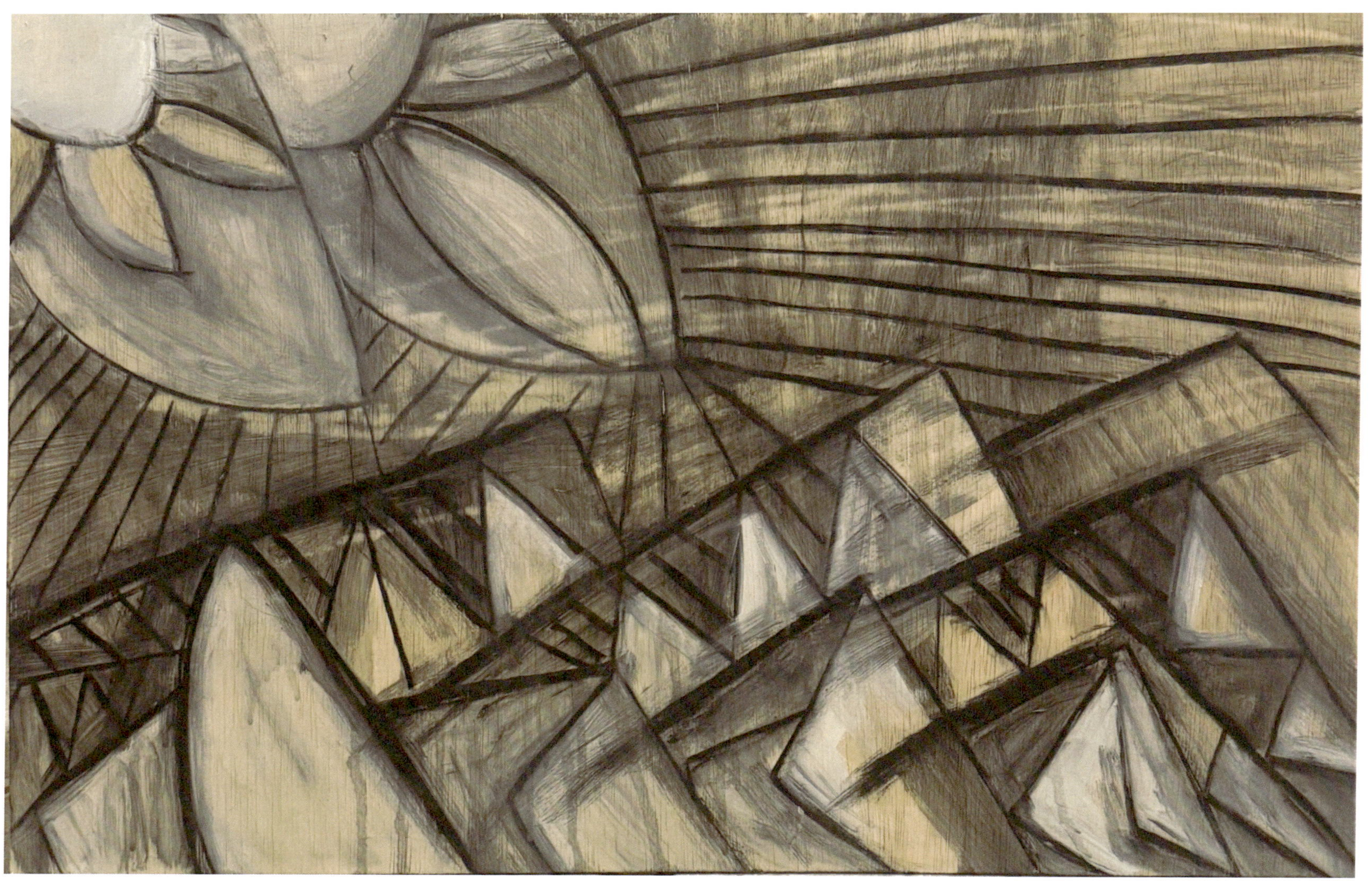

Mine FLowers

Oil, charcoal, laquer, on wood panel
16"x24"
2024

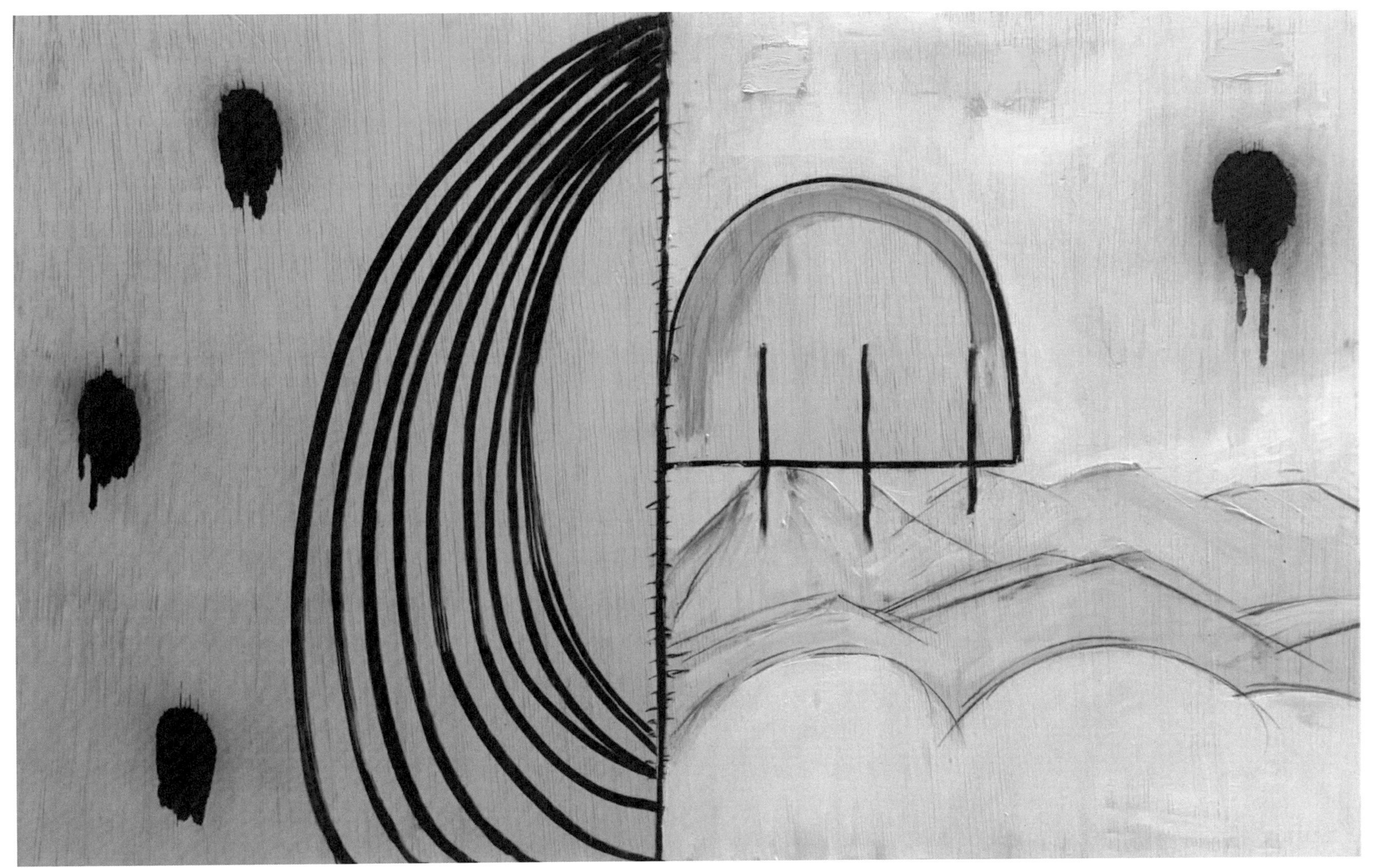

Kenslo

Oil, charcoal, on wood panel
16"x24"
2024

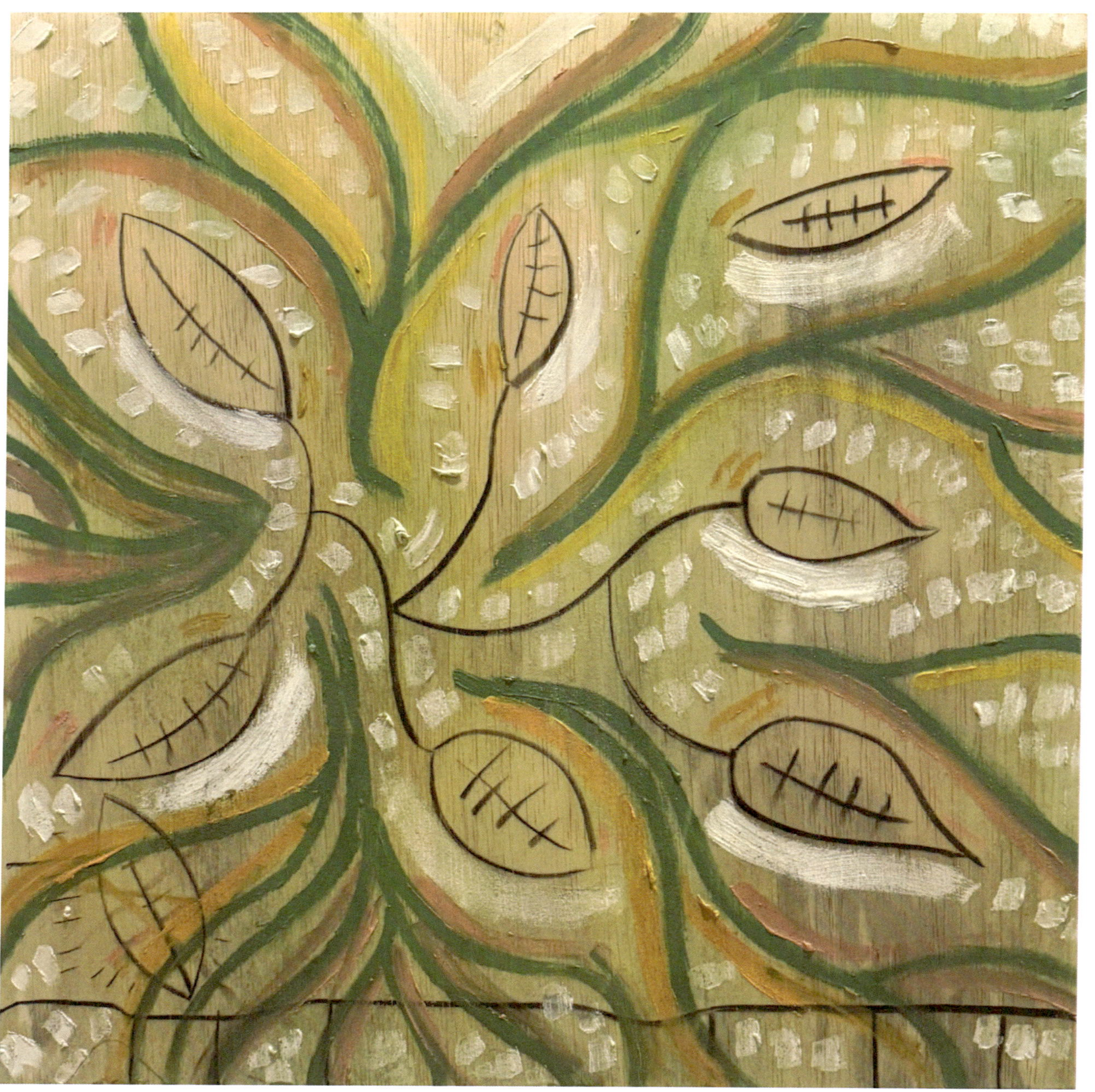

Garden #2
Oil, charcoal, laquer, on wood panel
16x16"
2024

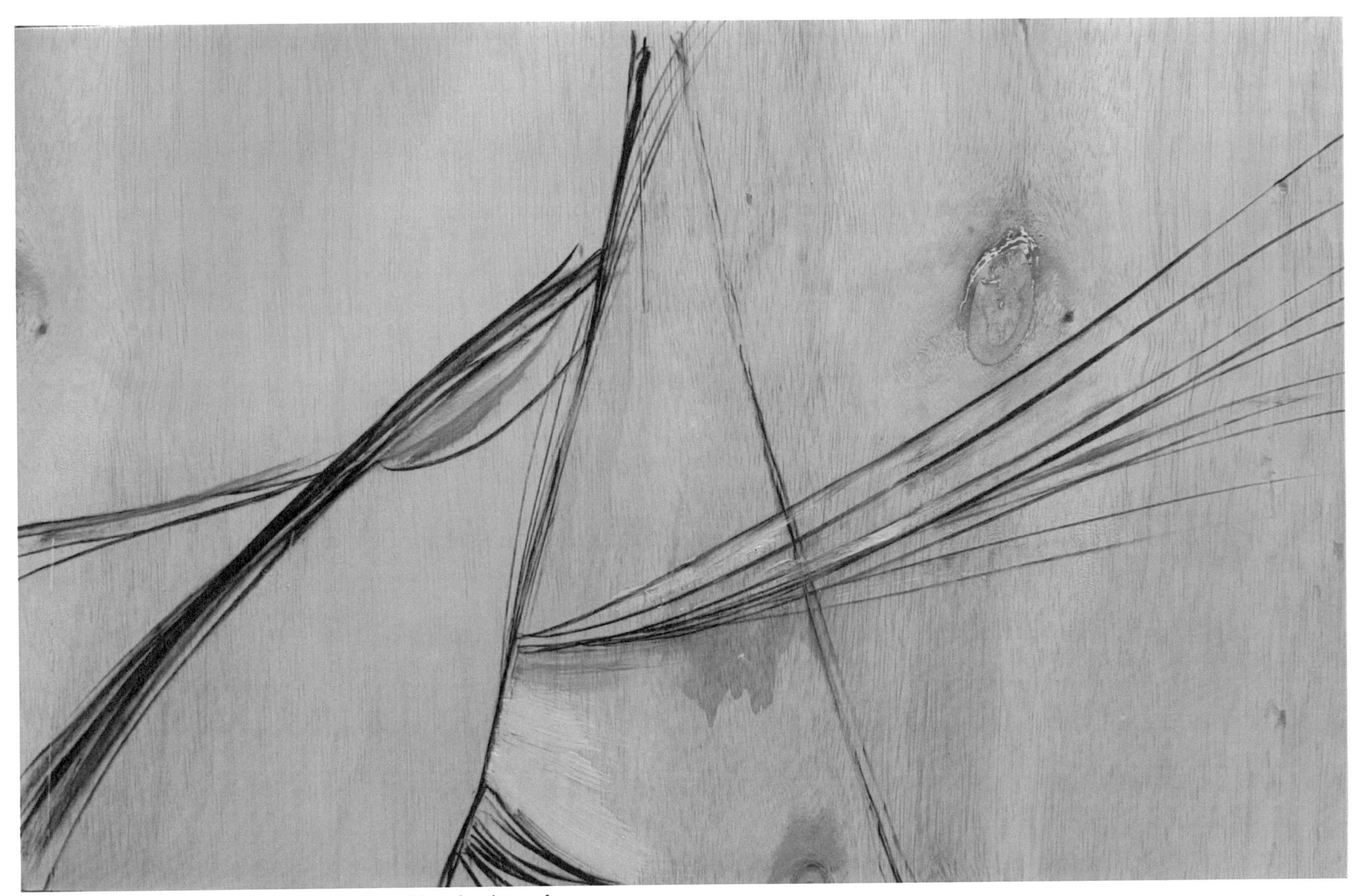

sometimes i put on glenn gould and paint and

remind myself beauty still exists.

Charcoal, oil, laquer, on wood panel.
16"x24"
2025

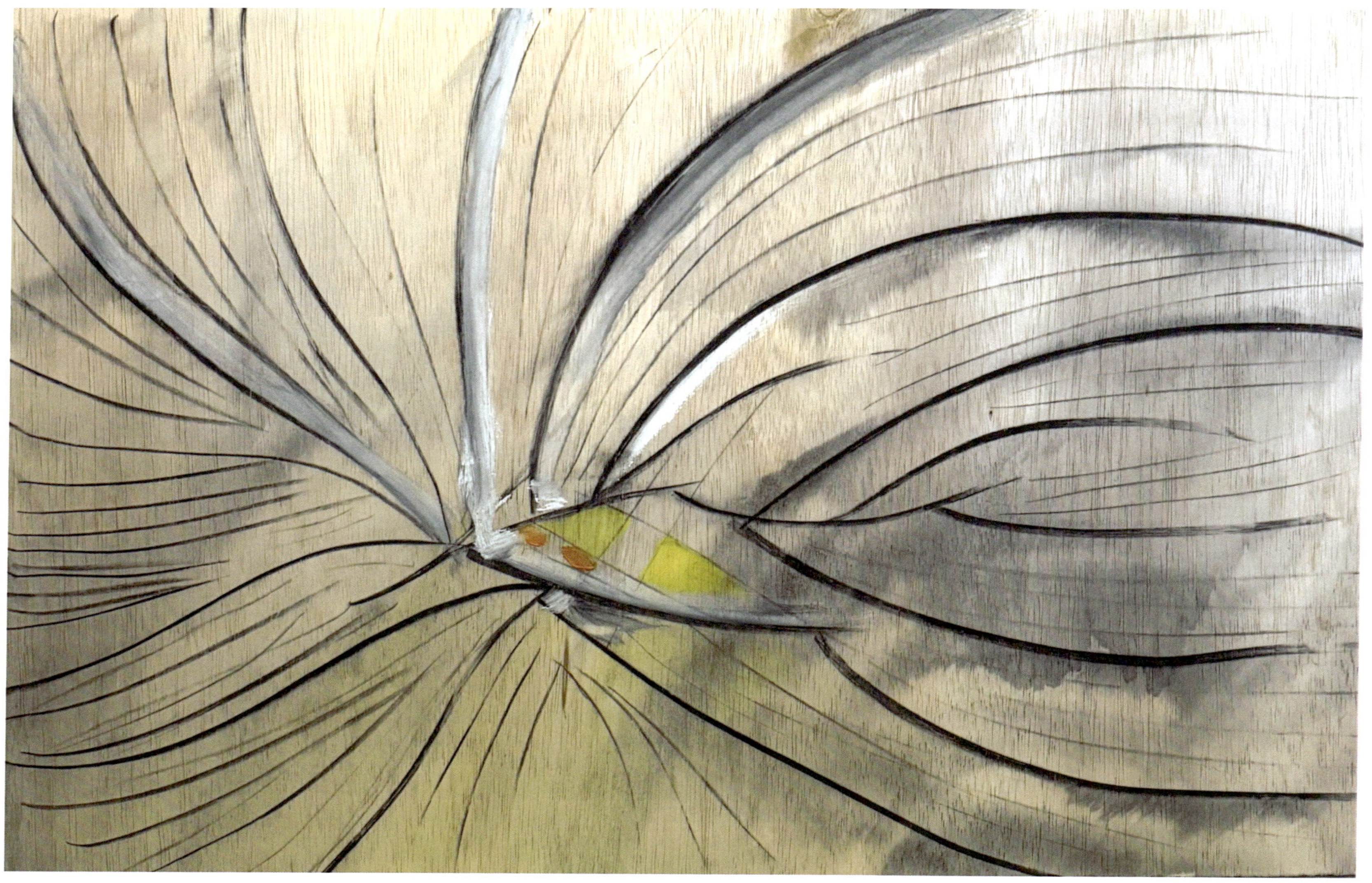

Ersu

Oil, charcoal, laquer, on wood
panel
16"x24"
2025

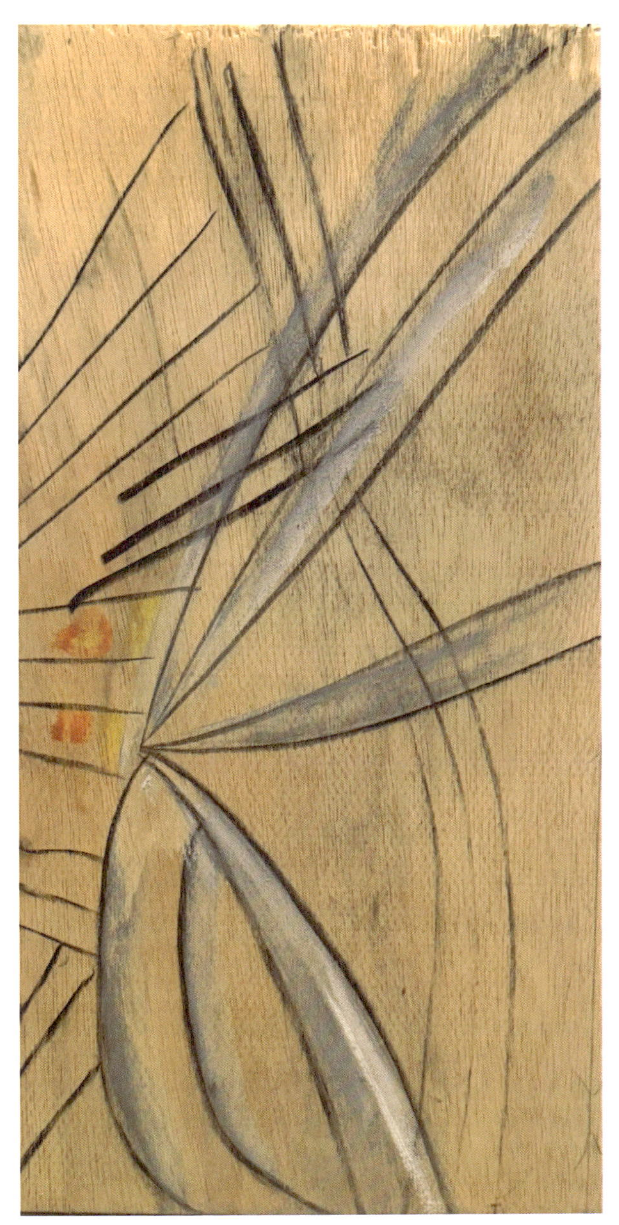

Mini Ursu

Oil, charcoal, laquer, on wood panel
8"x16"
2025

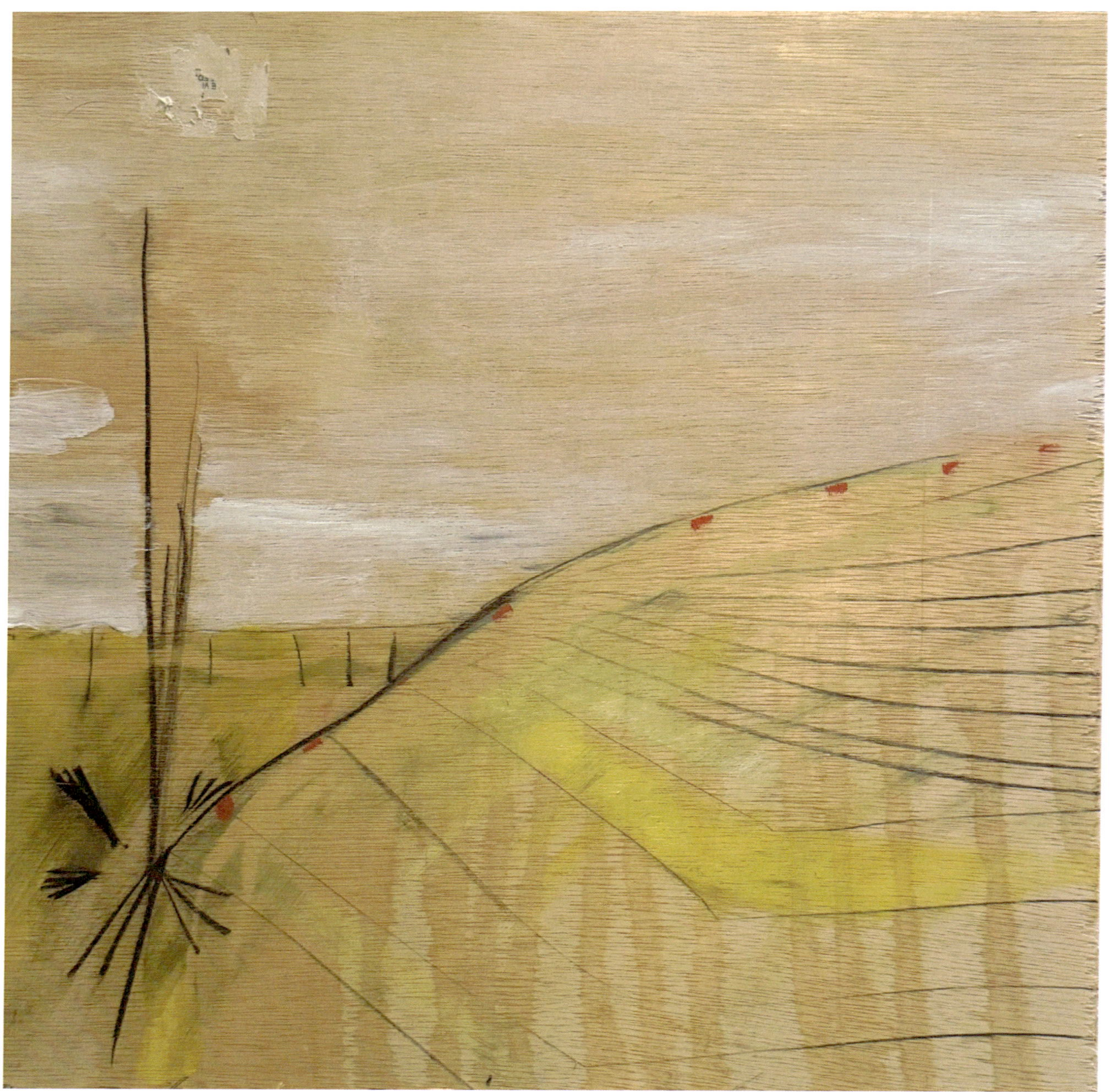

Piku

Oil, charcoal, aerosol, laquer, on
wood panel
16x16"
2025

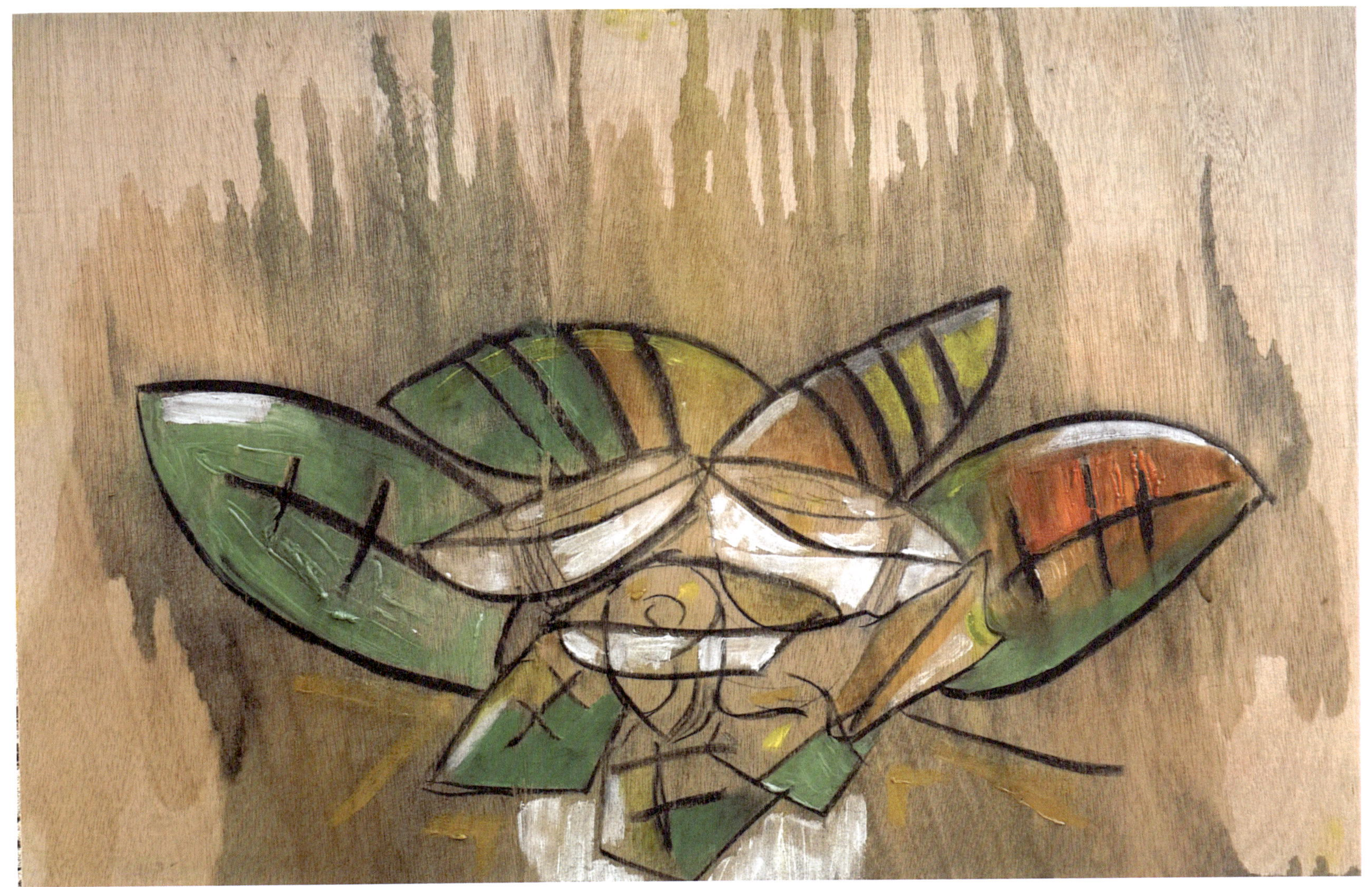

Kindlo

Oil, charcoal, laquer, on wood panel
16"x24"
2025

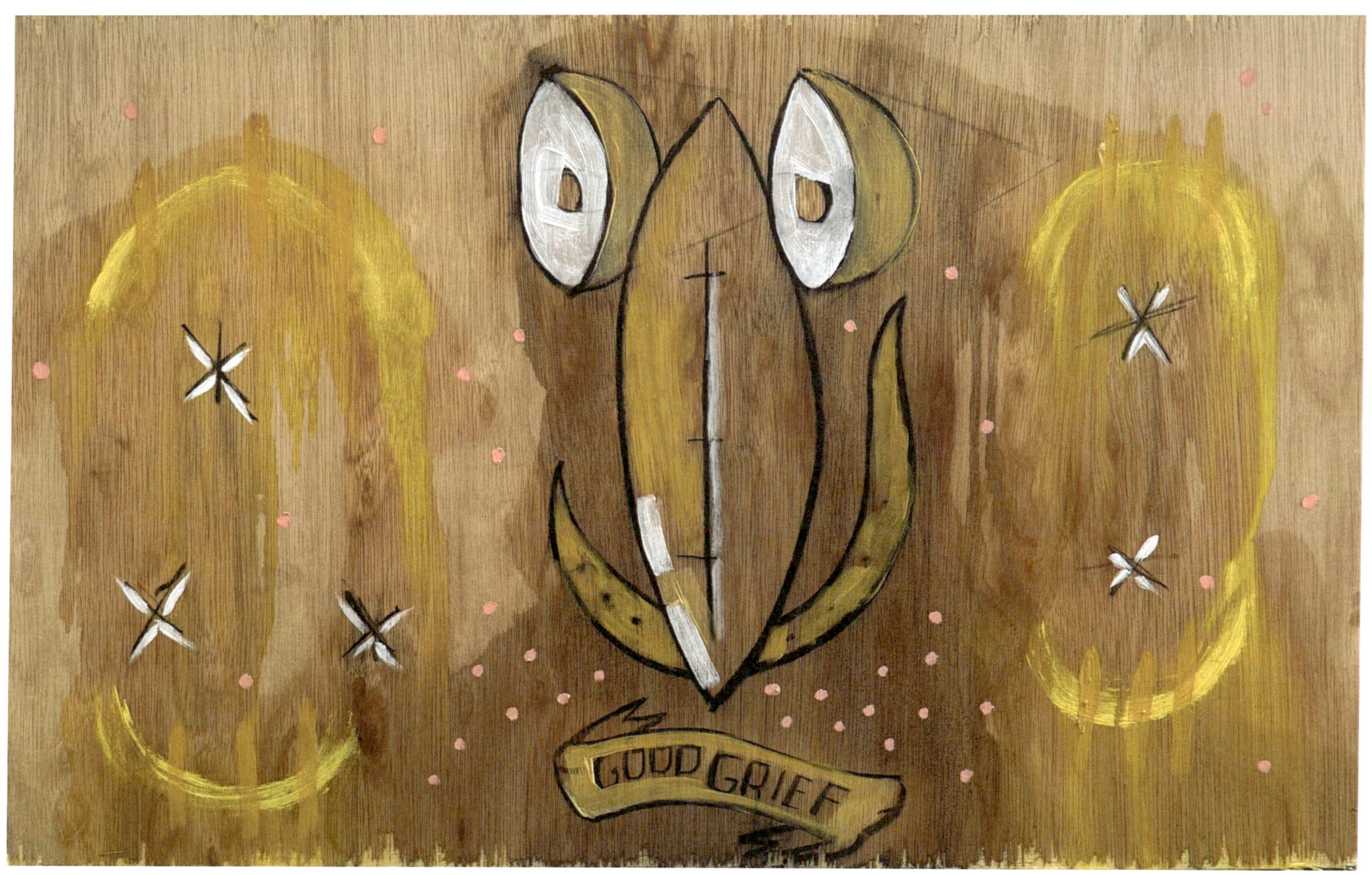

Good Grief
Oil, charcoal, laquer, on wood panel
16"x24"
2025

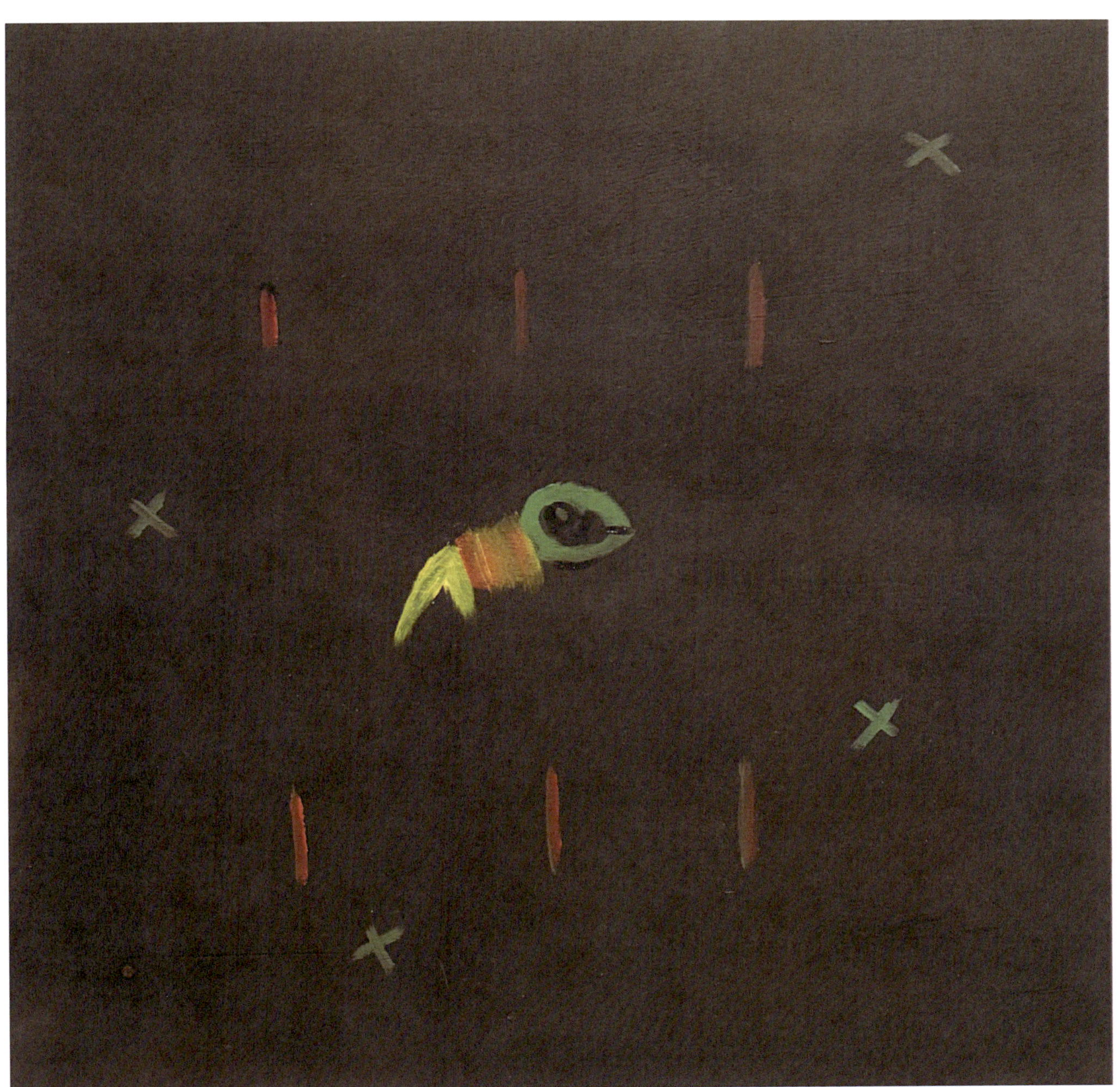

a beginning

Oil, aersosol, on wood panel
16"x16"
2025

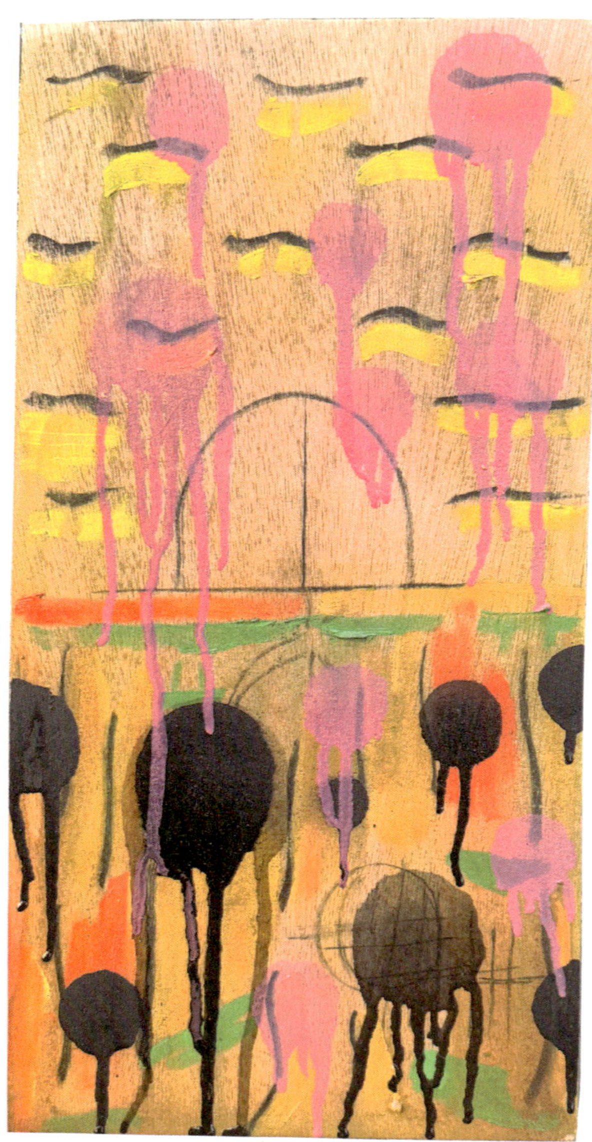

Ledo

Oil, charcoal, aerosol, on wood panel
8x16"
2025

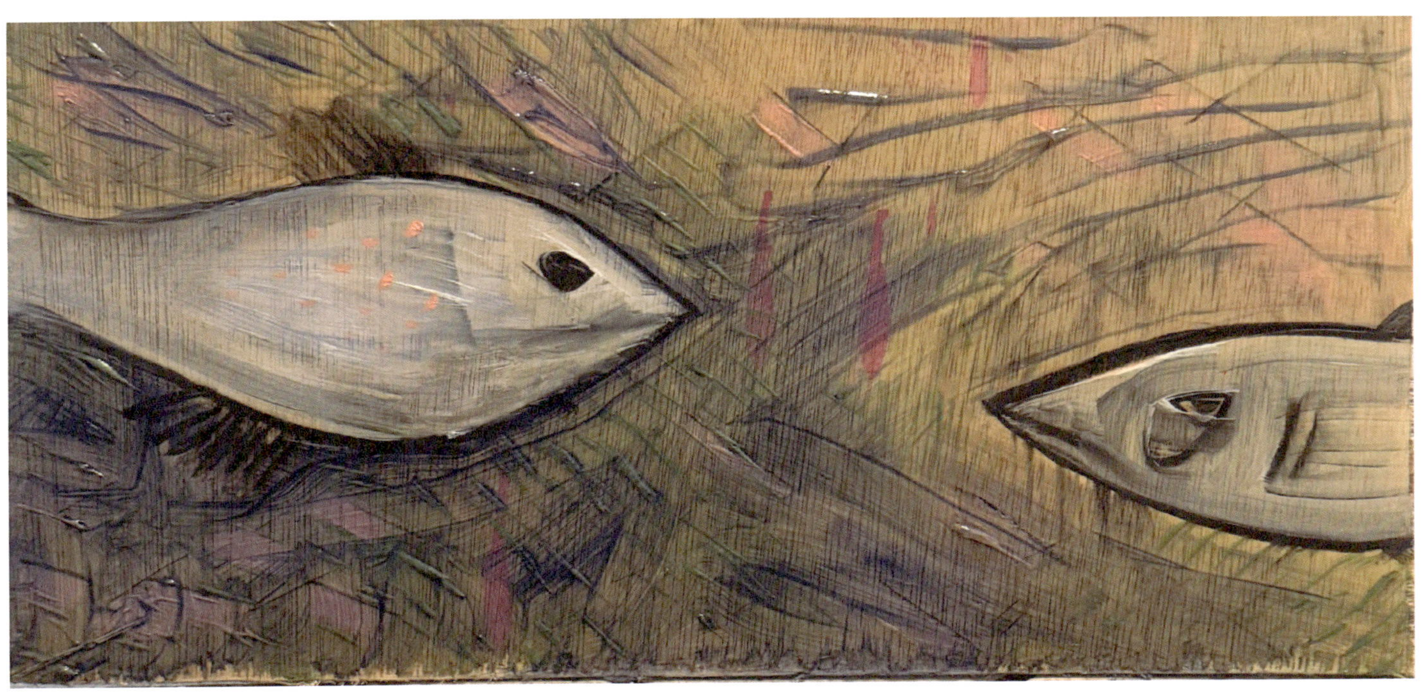

Fish-0

Oil, charcoal, aerosol, on wood
panel
8"x16"
2025

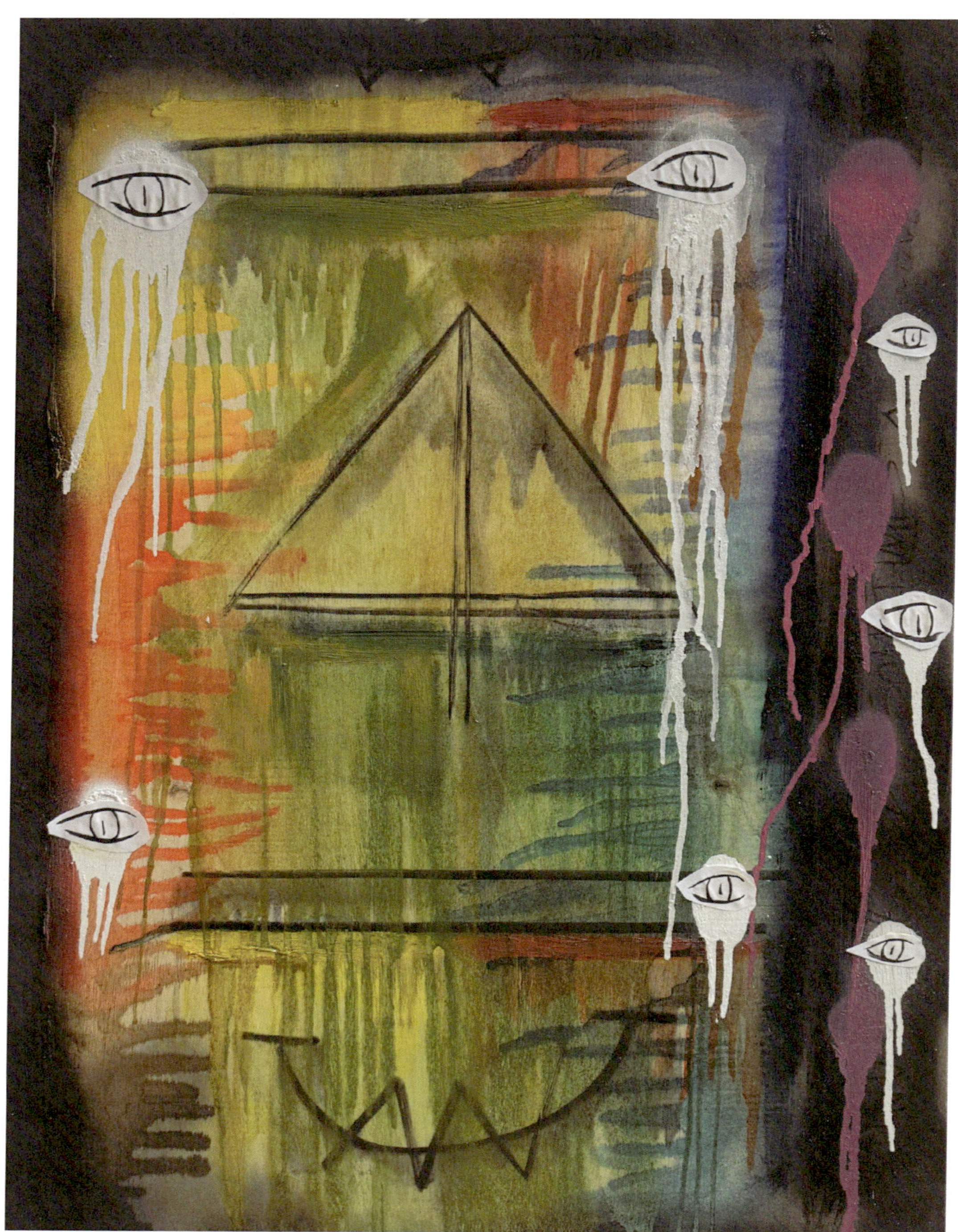

rrrr

Oil, charcoal, laquer, aerosol, on
wood panel
32x24"
2025

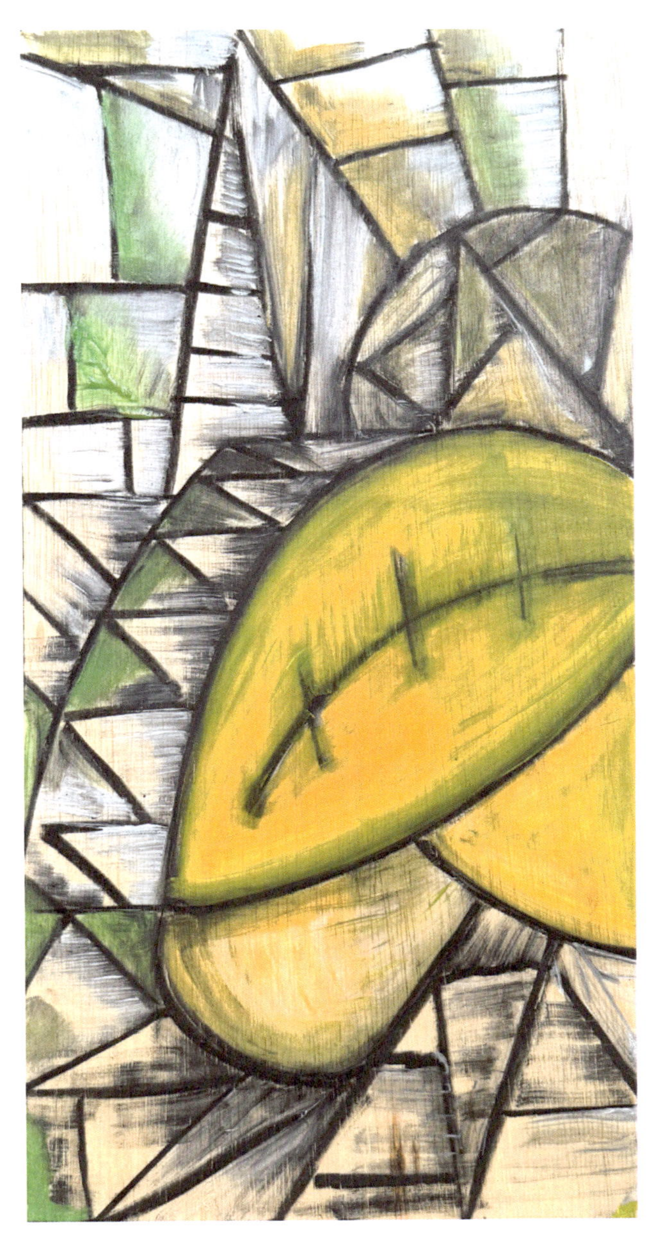

sh-ish

Oil, charcoal, laquer, on wood panel
8"x16"
2025

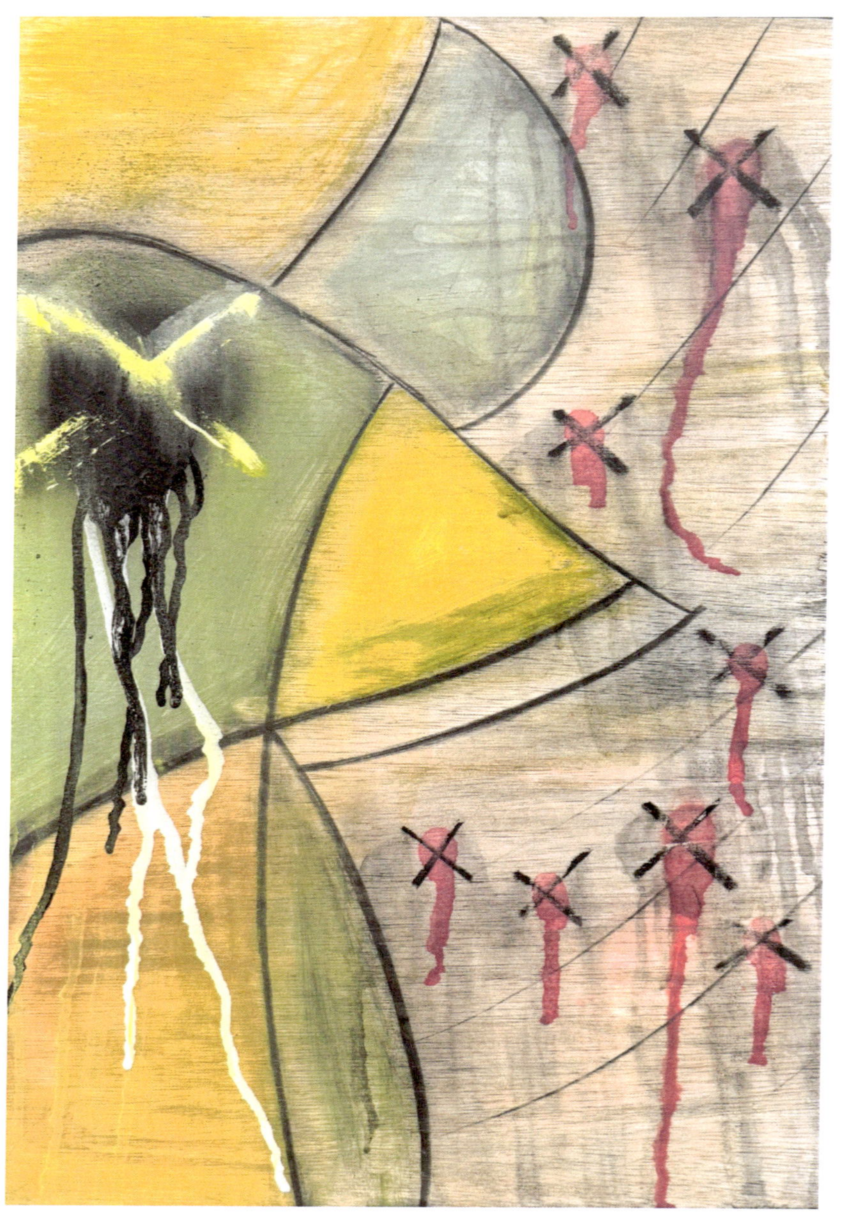

brkr

Oil, aerosol, laquer, charcoal, on
wood panel
16x24"
2025

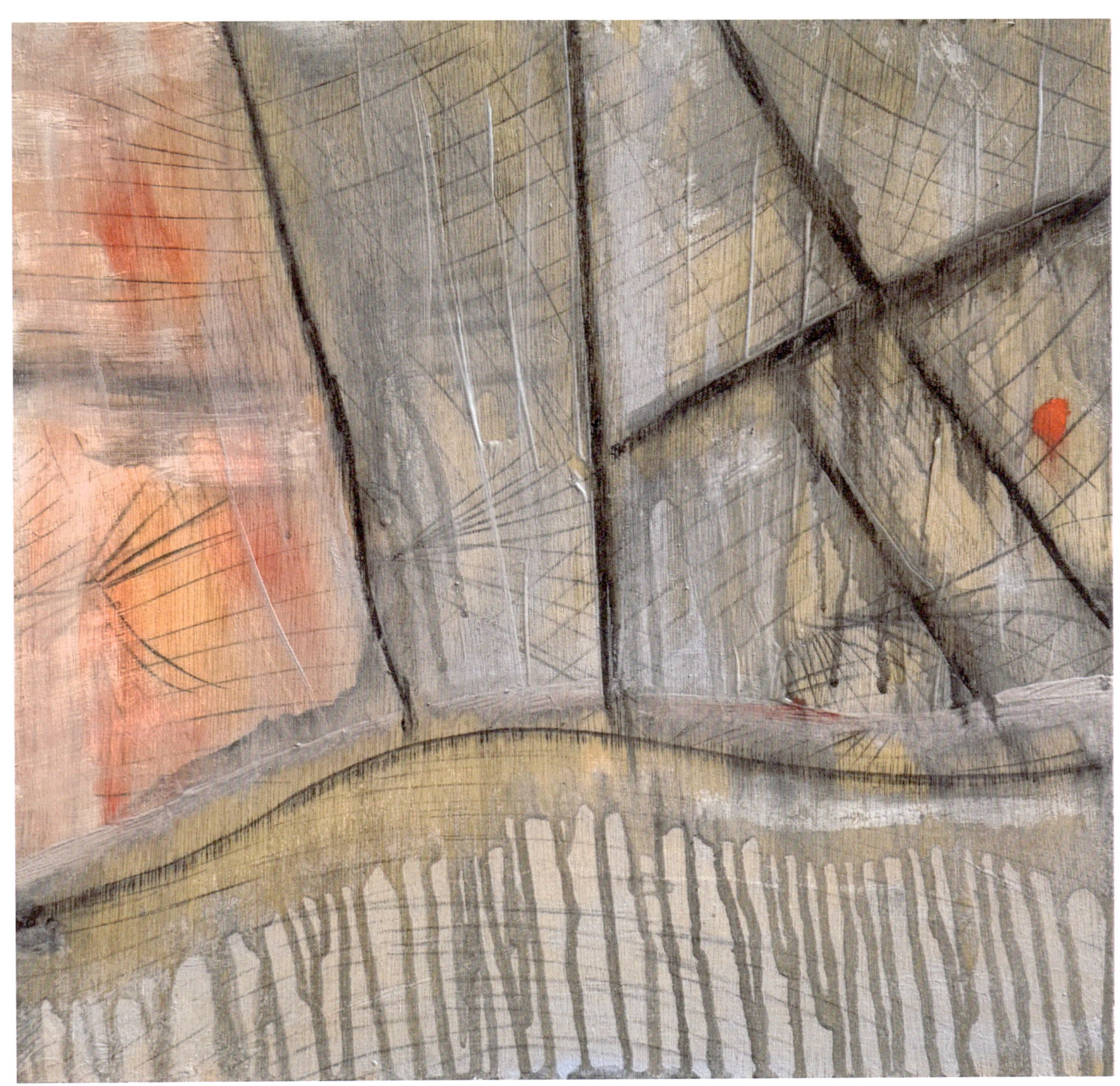

Ergo
Oil, charcoal, laquer, on wood panel
16"x16"
2025

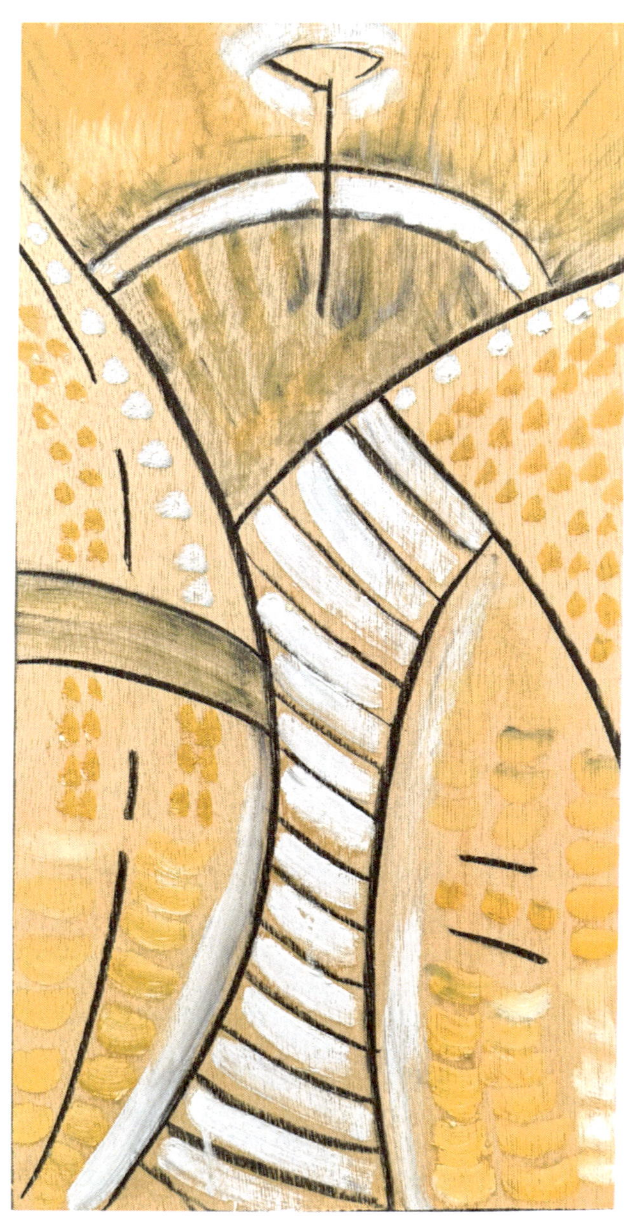

Face-r

Oil, charcoal, on wood panel
8x16"
2025

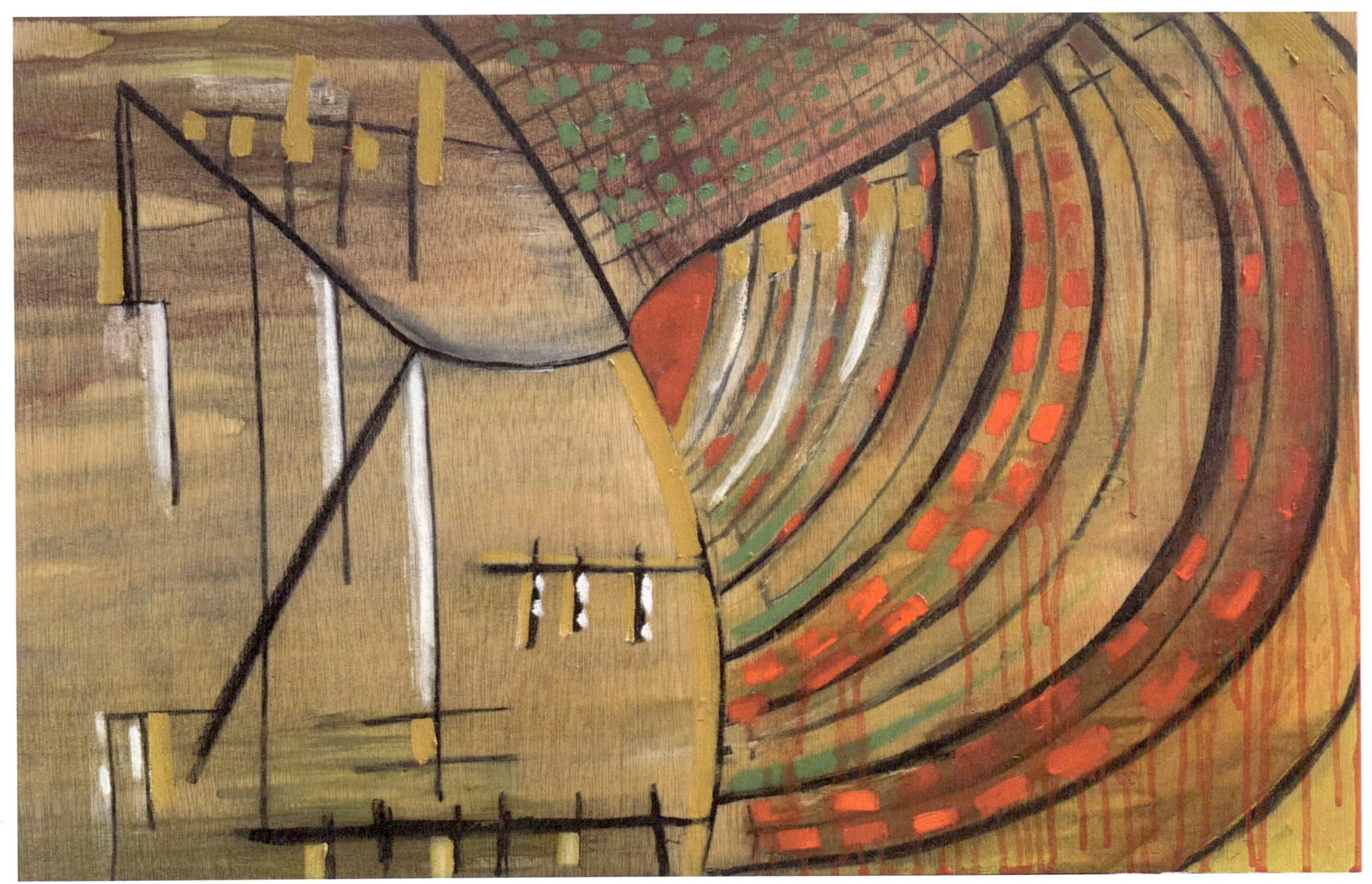

way it is

Oil, charcoal, laquer, on wood panel
16"x24"
2025

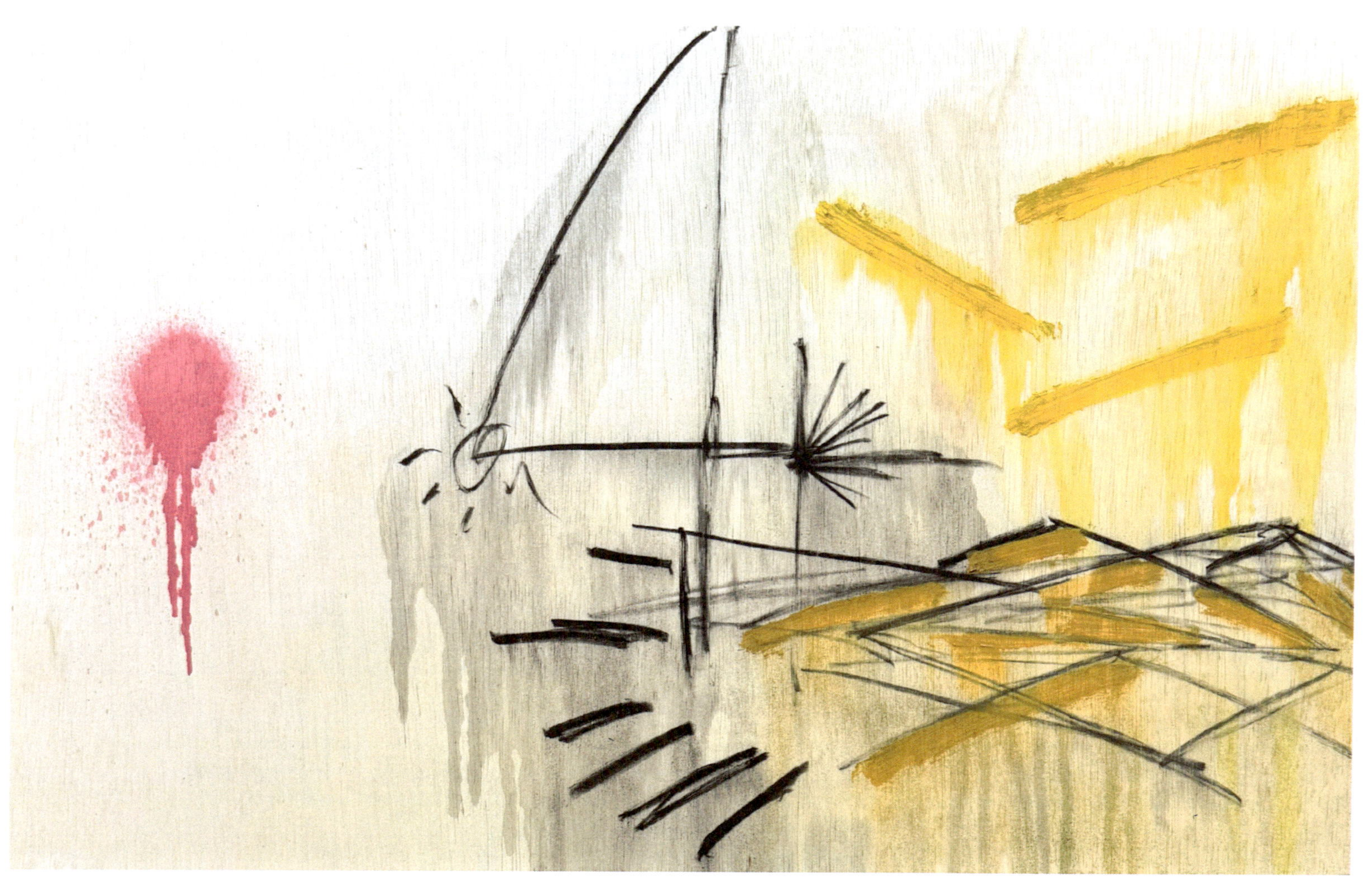

nothing really makes any sense at all
Oil, charcoal, aerosol, laquer, on wood panel
16"x24"
2025

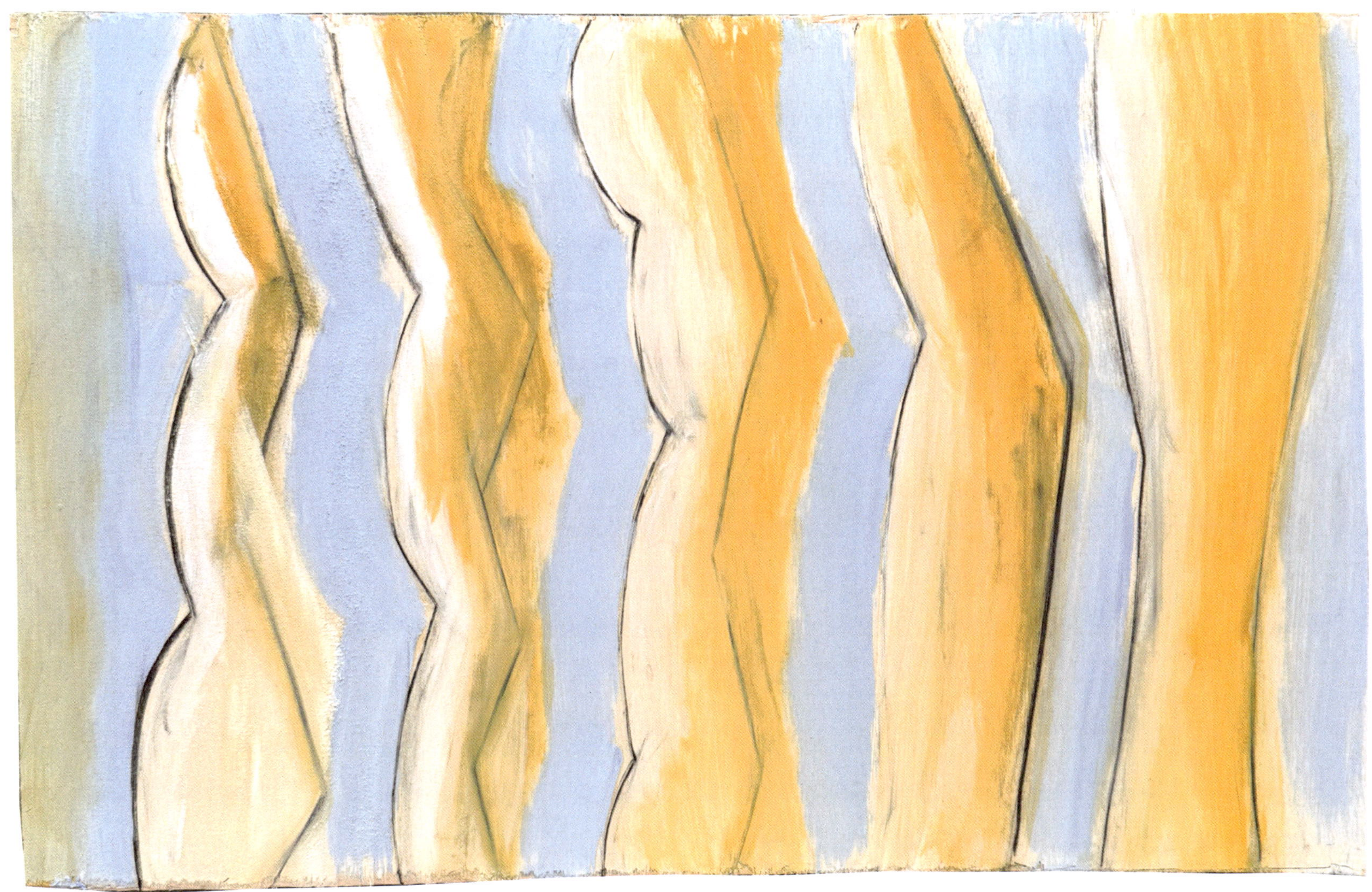

BKO

Oil, charcoal, on wood panel
16"x24"
2025

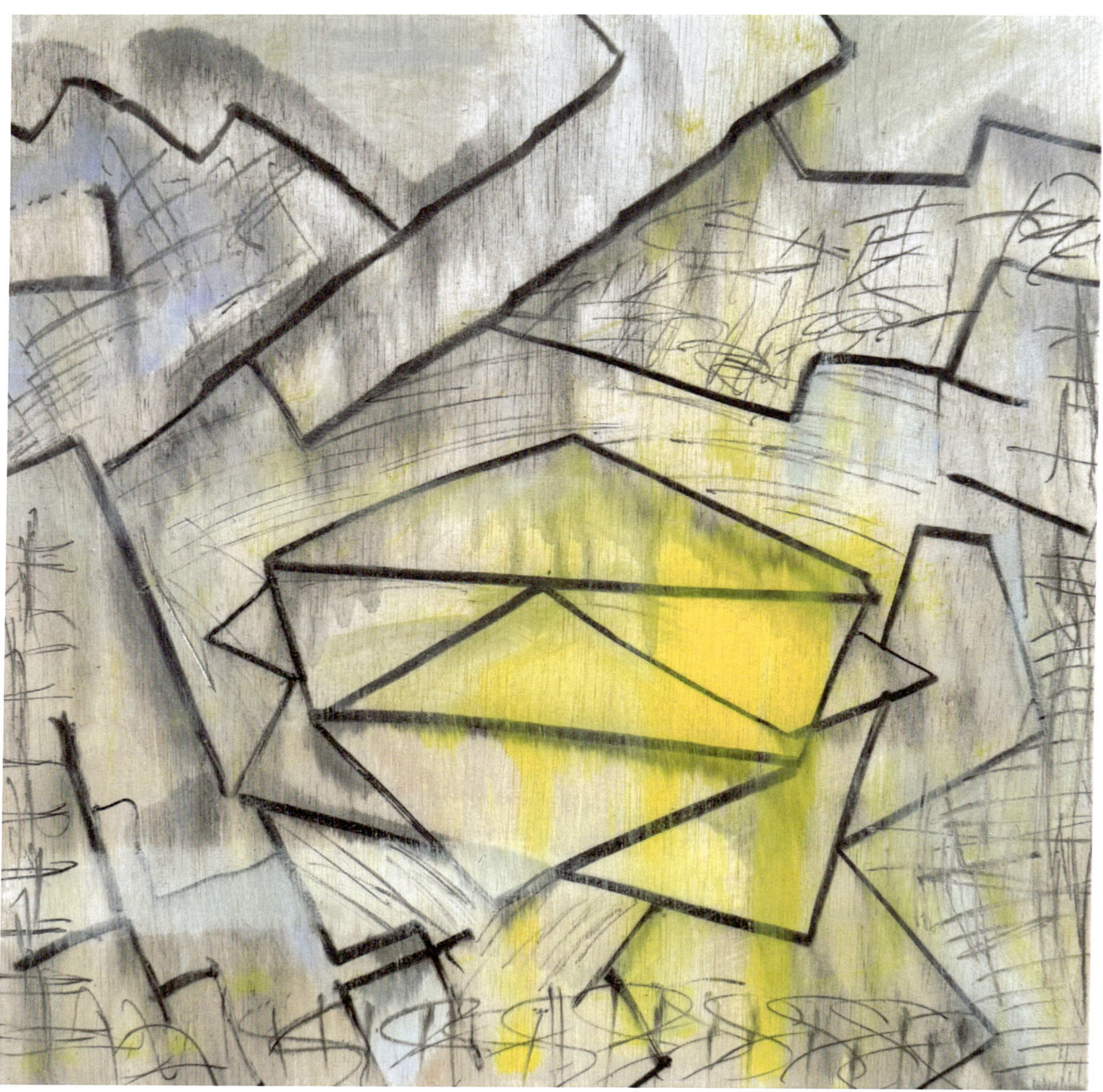

Rock

Oil, Charcoal, Laquer, on wood
panel
16x16"
2025

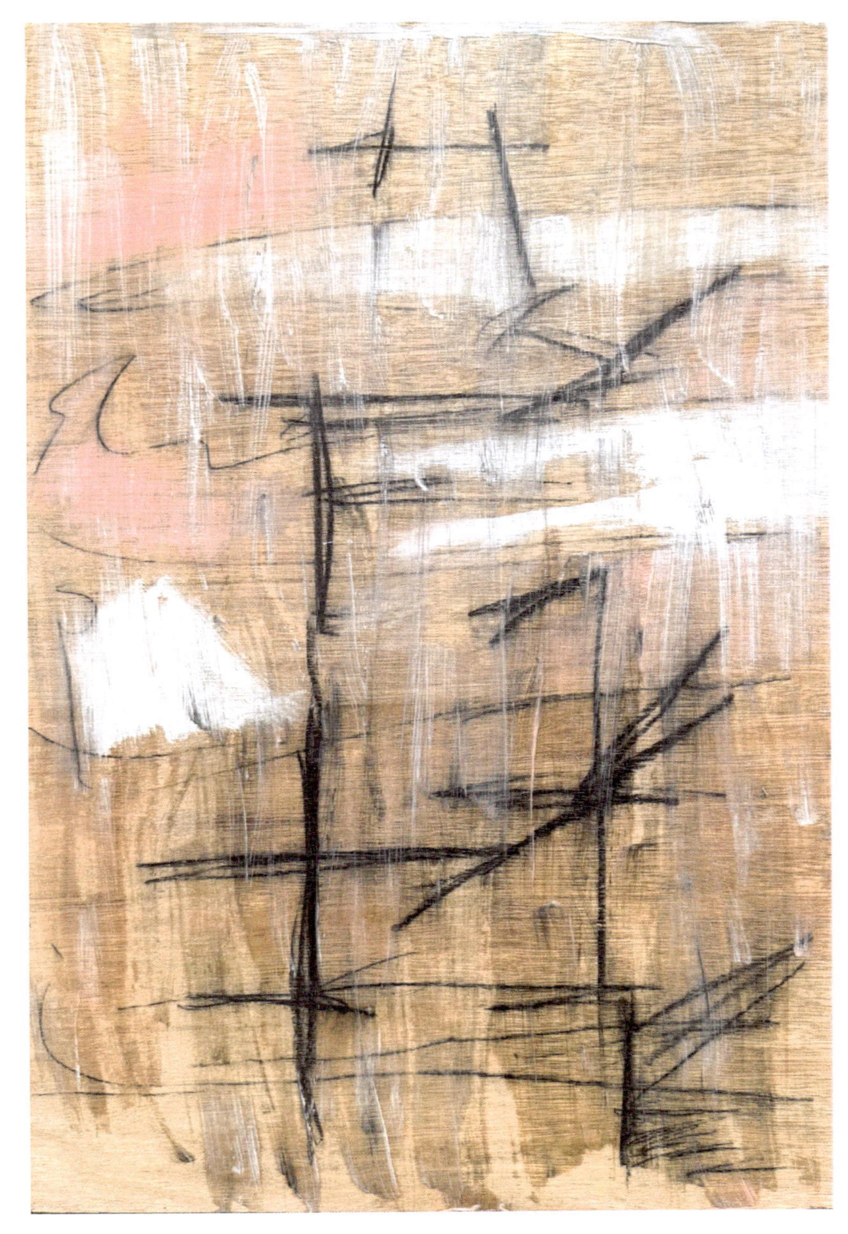

Casino

Oil, laquer, graphite, on wood panel
16"x24"
2025

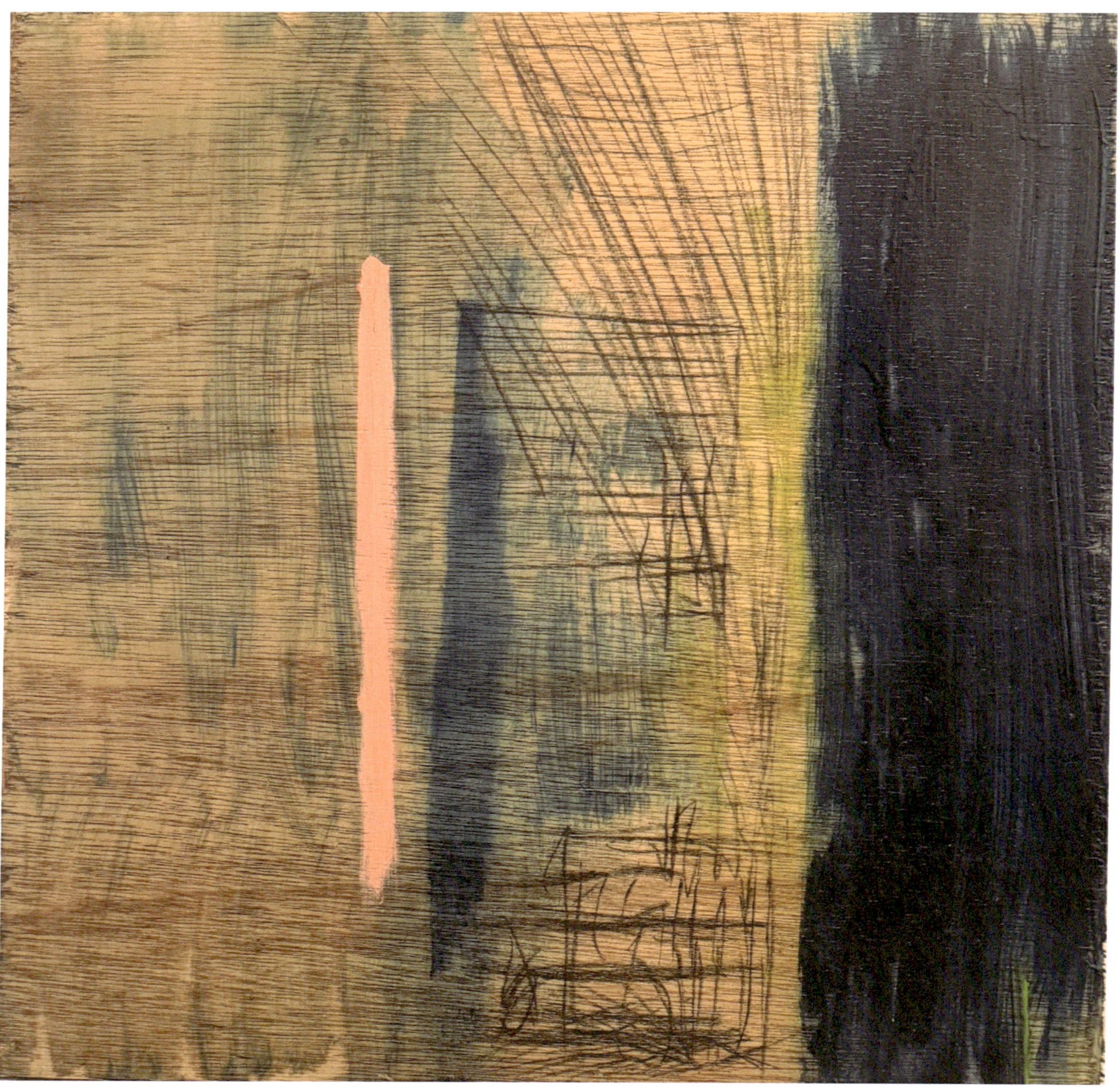

bkr

Oil, graphite, laquer, on wood panel
16x16"
2025

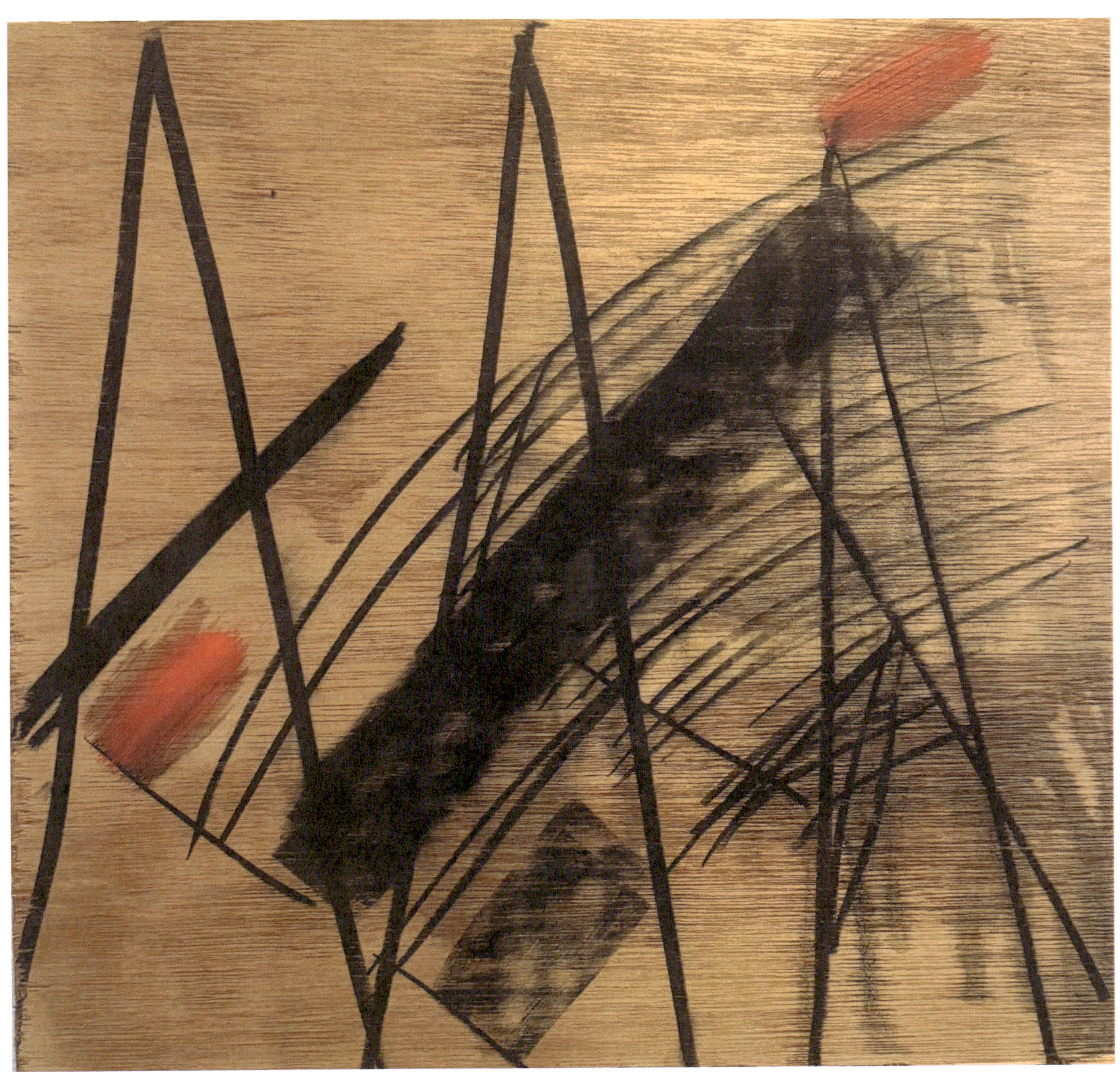

with, will

Oil, charcoal, laquer, on wood panel
16"x16"
2025

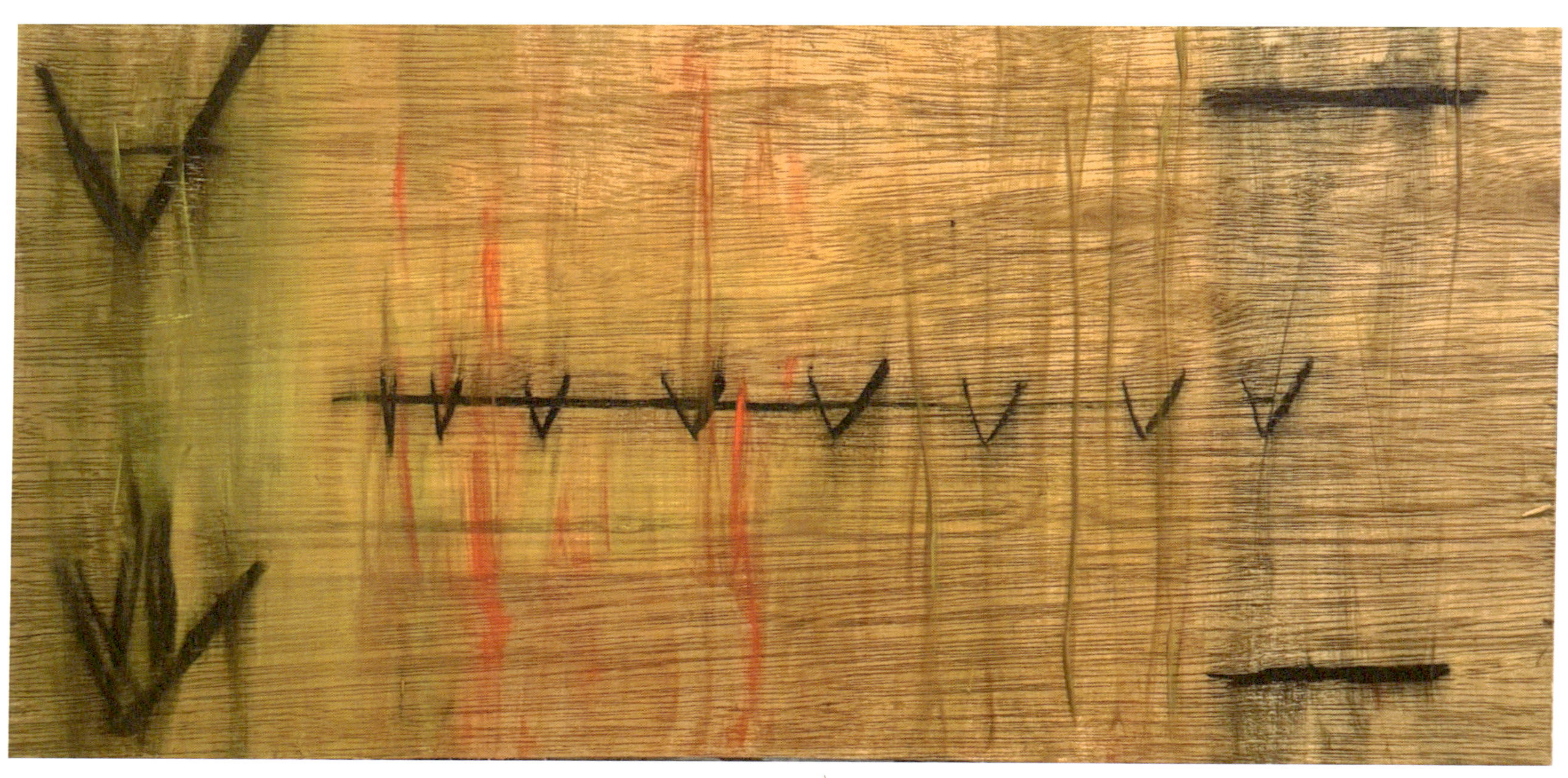

Provence

Oil, charcoal, laquer, on wood panel
8x16"
2025

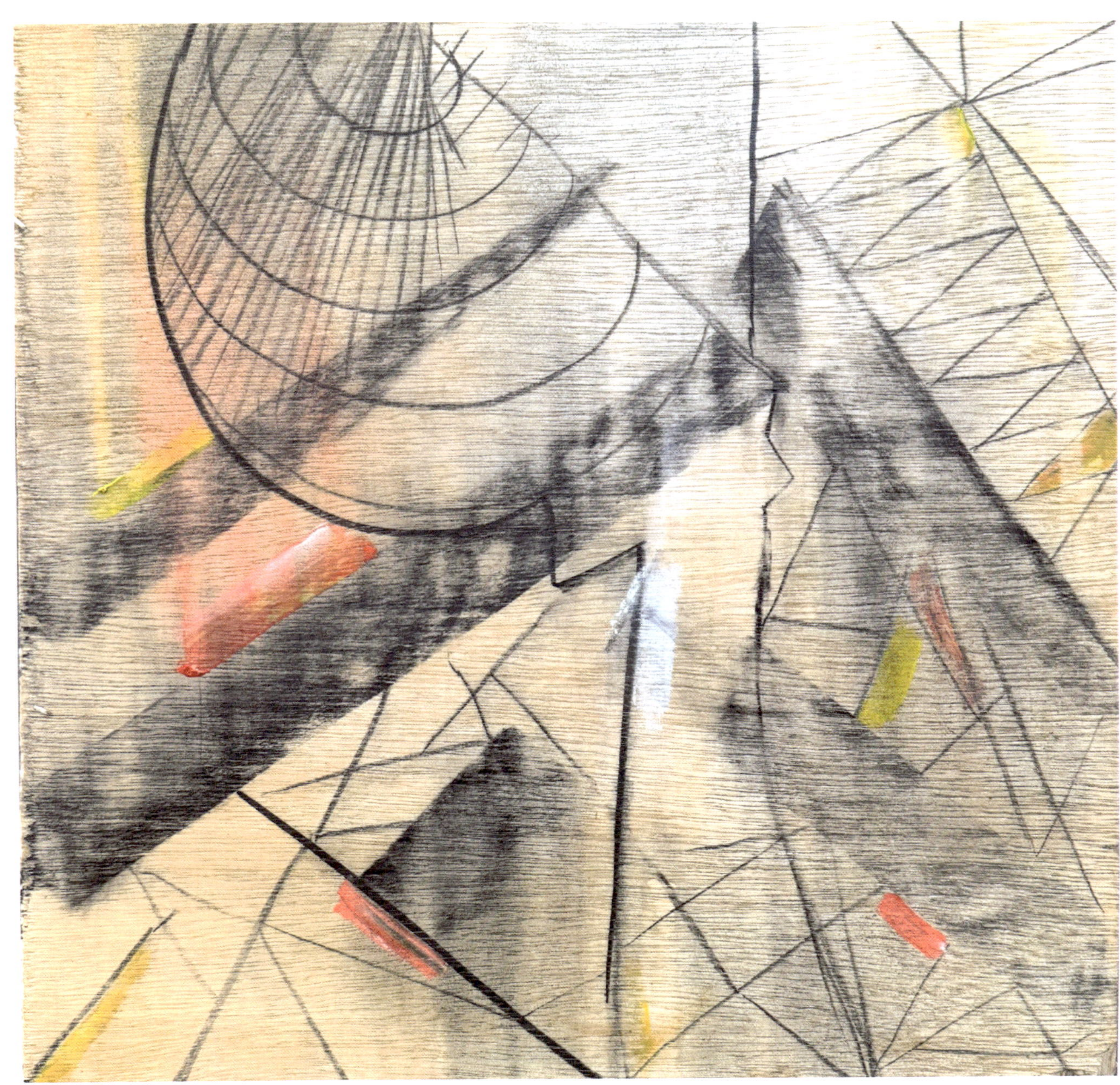

bno

Oil, charcoal, laquer, on wood panel
16"x16"
2025

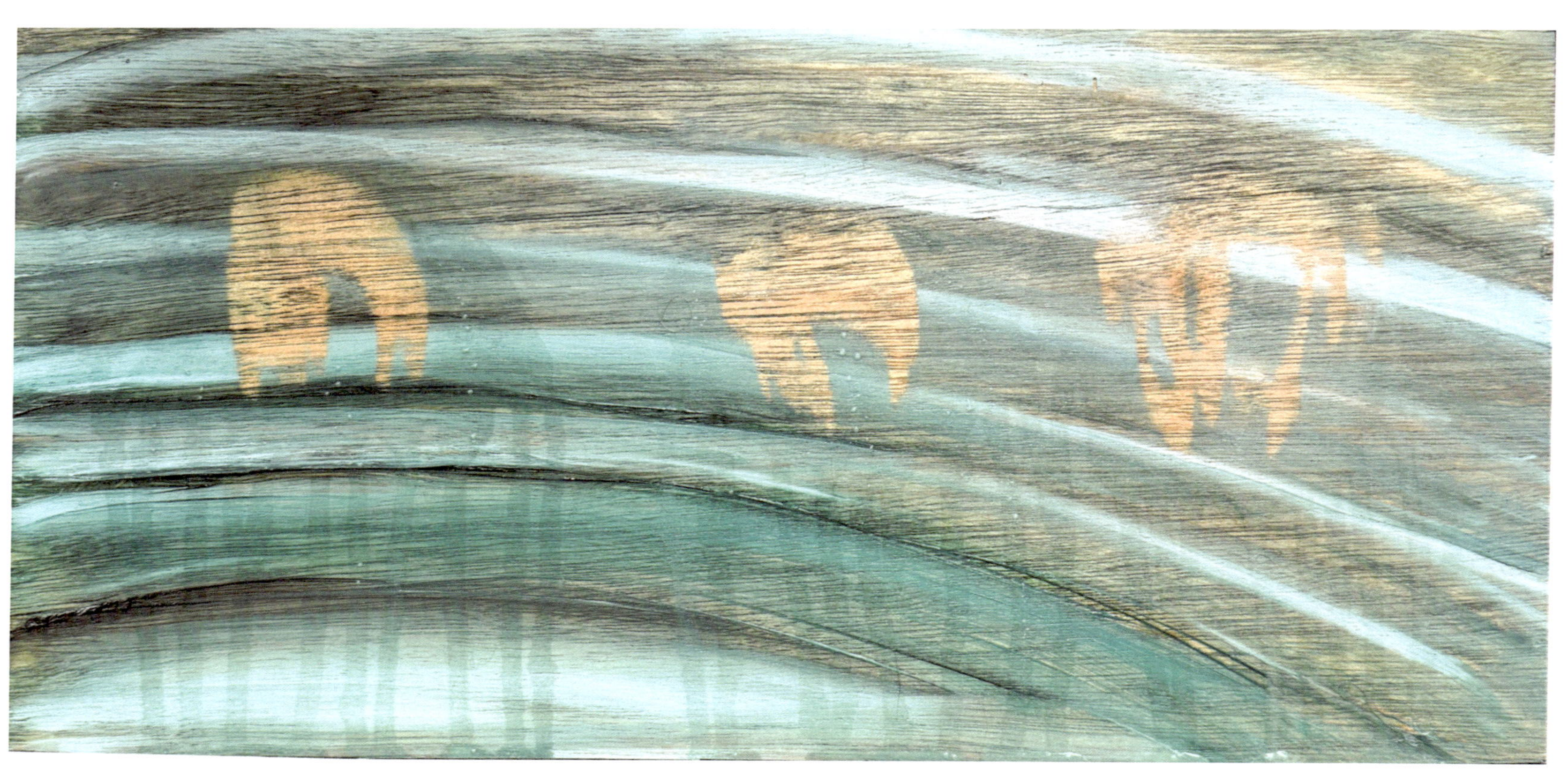

Portal
Oil, laquer, on wood panel
8x16"
2025

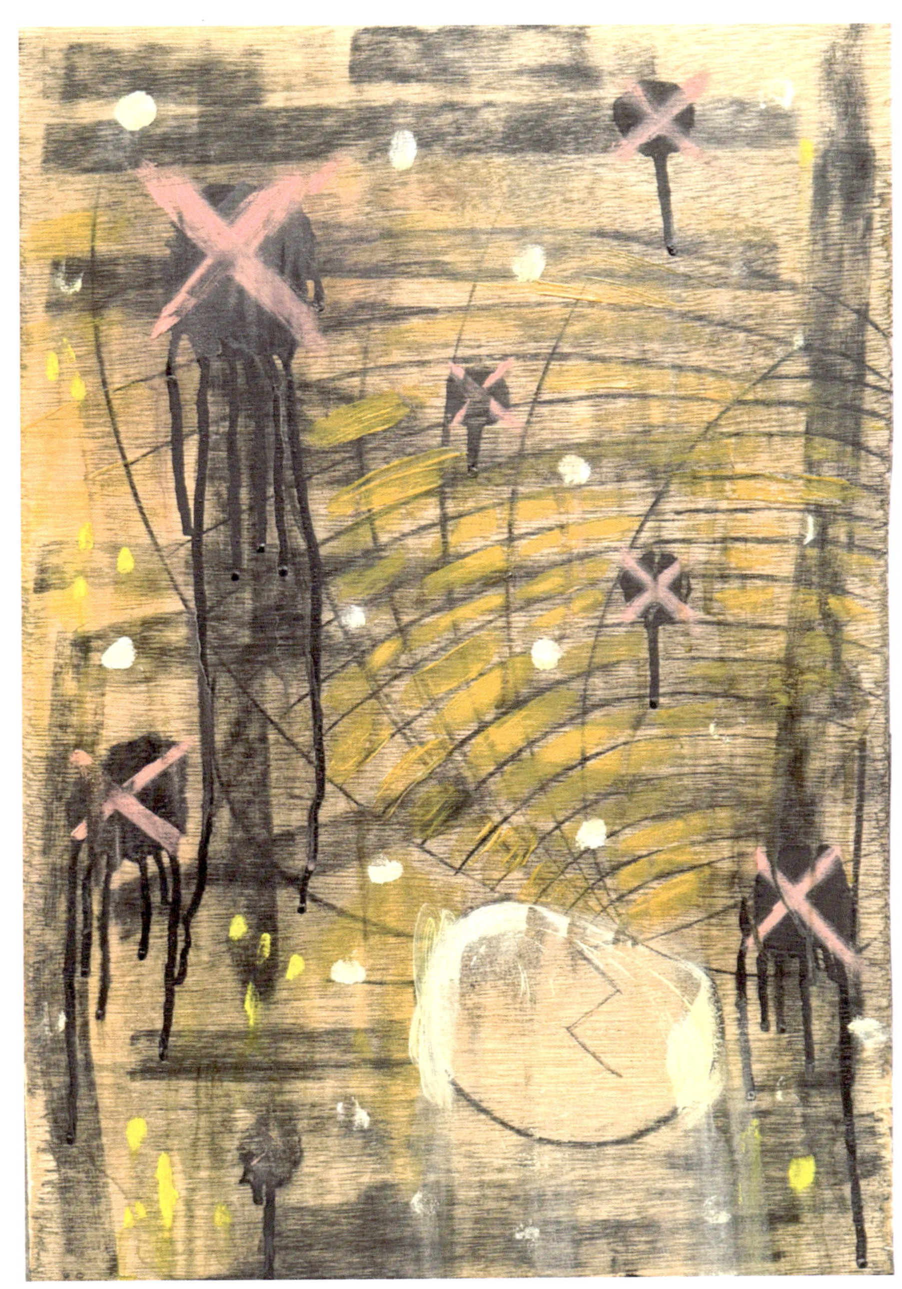

xa

Oil, charcoal, laquer, on wood panel
24"x16"
2025